# CATSKILL CRAFTS

# CATSKILL CRAFTS

## ARTISANS

## OF THE

## CATSKILL

## MOUNTAINS

by Jane Smiley

CROWN PUBLISHERS, INC. NEW YORK

Published by Crown Publishers, Inc.,
225 Park Avenue South, New York, New York 10003
and represented in Canada by the Canadian MANDA Group
CROWN is a trademark of Crown Publishers, Inc.
Manufactured in the United States of America
Library of Congress Cataloging-in-Publication Data
Smiley, Jane.
Catskill Crafts
1. Handicraft—New York (State)—Catskill Mountains
Region. I. Title.
TT24.N7S65   1987      745′.09747′38      87-899
ISBN 0-517-56700-8
10   9   8   7   6   5   4   3   2   1
First Edition

*for Phoebe and Lucy*
*and Willa and Max,*
*that they may put their hands*
*to good use.*

# Contents

# P r e f a c e

Every journalist needs to have an interview subject who takes her to task over the intentions, scope, and method of the project on which she is working, and I was fortunate to have such a subject in Henry Cavanagh, a ceramist profiled below, who told me right off the bat that writing the book I intended to write was "like talking to a rookie policeman in a bar and coming out with an eight-volume set called *Police Story.*" He's right. Then he said, "I'm a booster of what I think of as a local, or perhaps regional, phenomenon, and I want to see somebody do it justice. This is a snowball made from the tip of the iceberg. I have a sense of a true breadth of the subject. You are tapped into something that is incredibly rich and shouldn't be slighted or trivialized, but probably can't be done justice to. Statistically, there are more artists, however you want to define that term, living in Ulster County than in the rest of New York State, outside of Manhattan. I think there are a hundred and fifty artists you should see, seventy-five you must see, fifty you can't do without, and you're only interviewing twenty-five or so." And I agree.

The following book is by no means exhaustive, representative, or even selective. I bring to the work of these craftspeople no judgment except appreciation and no training except long interest. This book should instead be seen as a sort of friendship quilt, something like the banner of the Catskill Mountain Quilters' Guild, which contains squares representing scenes in the Catskills made by each member of the Guild and quilted by the group. Some are pieced, some appliquéd, all differ from the others in style and color, but the whole banner offers a picture. This book is a picture of the way some people are living, and earning a living, in a particular place at a particular time, that is, 1986. I happen to think that the place and the people and the way they live are of more than ordinary significance for a number of reasons, and so I offer this book. I offer it with a pleasure to people who love the Catskills, whether they have ever been there, or have only seen photographs. I offer it with thanks to everyone who helped me put it together: Harold Delucantonio of Fleischmanns, Ellen Schneider of Fleischmanns, Ed Fodor of Fleischmanns, Lumen Searle of Fleischmanns, Pauline Vos of Highmount, Howard Raab of Margaretville, Janis Benincasa of Margaretville, Shelley Postma of Pine Hill, Nancy Smith of Pine Hill, Robert and Anne Jones of Walton, Larry Bauer of Big Indian, Thom and Mary Klika of Boiceville, Betty Mac-Donald of Woodstock, Barry Miller of Woodstock, Barbara Goffin of Woodstock, Art Reed of Andes, to my friend, Annerieke Huismann and, especially, to all the members of the Catskill Mountain Quilters' Guild.

# CATSKILL
# CRAFTS

# Introduction

P eg, who has a baby-sitting business, often strips the quilt blocks together, because she doesn't feel that she can contribute her share to the quilting club by coming more often to the weekly quilting meeting. The most popular quilt colors are blues and browns, but this time she has chosen an unusual green, a muted sage color. The fabric must come from her scrap basket, because it feels like 100% cotton, soft and well washed. The twenty blocks were entries in a contest, the theme, "Flowers." Quilting groups often advertise quilt-block contests in the national quilting magazines. Quilters from all over the country send appliquéd or pieced patchwork blocks, and the best twenty are included in the quilt. Prizes are small, and the primary reward is in the work itself, of design and execution, as well as the knowledge that the work has been appreciated and chosen for inclusion in the quilt. For the Catskill Mountain Quilters' Guild, the resulting quilt is a product as well as a work of art—it will be raffled off or bid upon, and those funds will go into the Guild's treasury.

It is my first day at the quilting meeting, and I watch with interest as they put the quilt on the frame. A quilt frame consists of four long 1 × 2s clamped together at the corners with C-clamps and set upon four legs (or the backs of four chairs). First the quilt backing, a piece of green like the stripping, is spread over the frame and tacked down with push pins and thumbtacks. This will be a generous queen-sized quilt, about 7 feet wide and 9 feet long, so the frame takes up most of one end of the room. The batting is laid over the backing and gently smoothed down. In former times, quilters often used old blankets for the middle layer of a quilt, but now a number of companies produce sheets of lofty polyester fiber that is light, warm, and easy to stitch through. The batting is rough on top and bottom and stays put while the colorful, pieced top is laid over it and tacked through the backing to the 1 × 2s. The Catskill Mountain Quilters always begin with the frame open to its widest, quilting around the borders first and working toward the middle, though other theories yield other methods. Solitary quilters often set the quilt in the frame and roll it from both sides to the middle, or even from one side to the other, and then unroll it like a scroll as they finish sections of the quilting. But these quilters have the luxury of plenty of space for their meetings, so they don't have to compromise and risk puckering the quilt.

I have seen a lot of quilts, but I can't take my eyes off this one. Each of the twenty blocks is colorful and unique: The realistic appliquéd purple iris in the bottom row contrasts with the abstract green, pink, and white pieced representation of a rose in the second row. A tiny embroidered butterfly flutters around the sunflowers in the center. A lavender basket of flowers is beautifully defined by a great deal of painstaking embroidery. A traditional peony square in one corner con-trasts in style and tone with an original wreath design in the other corner. The dull green stripping is a restful setting for the bright, jewel-like colors of the squares. Nancy, the president of the quilters' guild, begins marking a pattern of interlocking hearts around the border of the quilt, as the others glance over from the quilt they are working on and make suggestions.

It is a peculiar summer for me. I am new in the area, and my house has no walls, no kitchen, no bannisters or railings protecting the drop from the balcony. The floors are single sheets of plywood; the lights, bare bulbs; the shower, a hose dangling out of sight of the road. I am far from my children and my friends, trying to build a house, finish a novel, and understand my life all at the same time. The only thing I do regularly is go to the weekly quilt meeting, and I always try to work on the flower quilt. I feel like I am stitching into it every bit of longing, frustration, and regret I have accumulated over the previous week. It gets more beautiful as we add each inch of white quilting against the green background. By the time it is finished, at the end of the summer, I can point out the parts of the border and the blocks that I quilted, and my work isn't bad—indistinguishable from the work of the other quilters, which is good enough.

And then it is Christmas, and I am back in the Catskills, having lunch with the quilt club. The house is finished, the children are with me, the novel is sold, the life, perhaps, understood. One child is eating cottage cheese, the other is wandering around the restaurant, and I am trying to listen to the conversation of the quilters and minimize damage to the restaurant at the same time. Although I have thought about the flower quilt often during the fall, and wondered how much they got for it, it is not until the last minute, just by chance, that I ask, "What was the final bid on that contest quilt from the summer?"

Nancy shakes her head. "We only got one bid."

"Are you kidding?"

"We hated to take it, it was so low."

I stop dressing the child for a second, and say, "What was it?" I am trying to figure out what can go unpaid for in the next few months.

"Three hundred."

Around the table, a chorus of renewed disappointment begins to rise. They know as well as I do that such a price is criminal for that beautiful piece of work.

I say, "This is low, too, but I would have given you four."

Nancy cocks her head. "We already—"

"It's in my purse," says Arlene, the treasurer. "I haven't mailed the acceptance yet. It's still in my purse. Isn't that amazing?"

It is not true, geologically, that the Catskill Mountains are distinct from the rest of the Appalachian chain, but the Catskills have always seemed self-contained—mysterious, beautiful, out of the way. Even now, no four-lane highway enters the heart of the region. Two-lane roads meander through small towns, where eateries and gas stations and shops line both shoulders. Smaller paved roads, gravel roads, and dirt tracks run back into the valleys and up the sides of the mountains. Access can be gained, but the sense of mystery isn't thereby lost—the woods are thick and shadowy, the valleys and declivities sudden and quiet. Although a hiker in the Catskills is never farther than three miles from a road or stream, he is also always close to what is normally hidden—common wood sorrel, growing under the leaves on the forest floor, wild turkeys roosting in a tree, white-tailed deer in a clearing, a timber rattler on a warm rock on the top of a mountain, a few brook trout in a small pool. Known but not domesticated, exploited but not destroyed, rural but cosmopolitan, the Catskill region is a region of paradoxes, and, in my view, it is the successful but tenuous balance of these paradoxes that gives the mountains vitality and the promise of being preserved in a time when human pressures on the countryside have become almost insupportable in other parts of the nation.

To begin with the basics: The Catskills may be arbitrarily defined as the region north of Route 17, west of the New York State Thruway, southwest of Route 145, and southeast of Interstate 88, as it runs from Binghamton to Cobleskill. The heart of the region is Catskill Park, a state park of some 650,000 acres that lies mostly in Ulster County and contains the Ashokan Reservoir, the Rondout Reservoir, and part of the Neversink, and runs along the south bank of the Pepacton Reservoir. All of the highest Catskill peaks are in the park—Slide Mountain, Hunter Mountain, Black Dome, Doubletop—and they all have about the same elevation—around 4,000 feet. Two towns, Kingston and Oneonta, define the eastern and western ends of the Catskills, and they aren't very large. Kingston has some 25,000 inhabitants, Oneonta, about 15,000. Otherwise, villages are small. Delhi, the county seat of Delaware County, numbers fewer than 3,500. Middleburgh has 1,400, Margaretville, fewer than 1,000. The Catskills are more rural, in their way, than places in farm states such as Iowa and Nebraska, meaning that the land is less settled, less developed, less exploited for agriculture.

Like most of eastern New York State, the Catskills were once privately owned, forming a large, complicated "patent," or land grant, and this partly accounts for the laggardly way in which they were settled—not in the seventeenth century, like New England and Virginia, but in the late eighteenth and early nineteenth, like Ohio and Kentucky. But it is also true that in many ways the Catskills repelled settlement. The land was steep, the climate cool, the mountains unpossessed of mineral wealth. Only a few types of farming were discovered to be possible: rye, cabbage, cauliflower, and milk each had their day, as did stripping of hemlock bark for tanning. During the nineteenth century, nearly all of the mature hemlock forests that covered the mountains were clear cut and stripped. The present sugar maple forest is an immature replacement forest, but relics of the hemlock forest can be seen at the tops of many Catskill peaks.

The Catskills are a place where people generally must choose to remain, because there is little in the way of economic incentive to keep them there or to bring them there. A generation ago, dairy farming was a living, if not necessarily a prosperous one, for many families and formed the economic base of the region. This is no longer the case. One of the craftspersons I interviewed commented on what, to me, is a startling fact—in the last ten or twenty years, land that was once pasture has been taken over by scrub and small trees—from her house above Highmount Ski Center, some 2,500 feet, Pauline Vos can see eleven miles to Roxbury. Since she has lived there, she has seen the dark green of the forest close over the light green of pasture. And one day at the quilters' meeting, Elsa Sanford, who was raised on a farm near New Kingston, mentioned driving up the valley toward her parents' farm for the first time in ten years, and being appalled by the disappearance of the pastures, and the views, of her earlier years. All the natives of the area went into a chorus of agreement—compared to thirty years ago, you can't see anything anymore. According to Janis Benincasa, the folklorist at the Erpf Center, one of the causes of the decline in dairy farming was the switch from Jersey cattle, who will climb hills in search of forage, to Holsteins (the common black and white dairy cow), who won't. Jersey milk, of course, has a much higher butterfat content than Holstein milk, the reason for the switch in the first place. In addition to this, many thousands of acres of river bottomland, the only land really flat enough for profitable agriculture, was condemned and then flooded to create the six New York City reservoirs.

Nonetheless, the ecological variety and vitality of this region have not been damaged here as elsewhere. For one thing, the region lies across the boundary of two types of forest—transition forest, which for the most part lies slightly to the north of the Catskills, and mixed deciduous forest, which for the most part lies slightly to the south. There is intense natural competition for every niche in the ecosystem, which means that the ecosystem as a whole, being various, is a healthy one. The depredations of human exploitation that result from crop monoculture and industrial pollution are absent from the Catskills, and much of the steepest, most fragile land is protected as a part of Catskill Park. Even acid rain, a significant problem just to the north, in the Adirondacks, affects the Catskills less, because of the nature of prevailing winds. Part of the reason I love the Catskills is the variety of wildlife—the casual visitor may see not only deer but wild turkeys strolling along the shoulder of Route 28, not only woodchucks and snakes and skinks but goldfinches and even eagles.

As much as any self-sufficient farming region, the Catskills have a craft tradition, especially a tradition of crafts associated with domestic life, such as quilting, and those associated with hunting, such as carving decoys and gunstocks and making game calls. There were, of course, local carpenters and furniture makers and blacksmiths. The craft of building covered bridges was highly developed during the nineteenth century, and many barns and other old buildings that still stand attest to local notions of design, as well as local skills. That handcrafts flourish in the Catskills in 1986, and look as though they will only continue to flourish, is partly due to this tradition—the Catskills are a place where crafts are understood and respected, where many people do something with their hands that their parents and grandparents did before them.

But the Catskills have accepted repeated infusions of outsiders from the beginning, and have never been so remote that native sons, once they found their way out, didn't come back. Since long before the Catskill School of painters, artists have found inspiration in the precipitous beauty of the mountains and waterfalls, and at least since the 1920s, they have found, in Woodstock, a place to live and work. When, in the late sixties and early seventies, numbers of college-age hopefuls set out to make their lives around art and craft and nature, Woodstock, and then more distant parts of the Catskills, were there to receive them. In some cases, the reception was a reluctant one, given the political climate of the time, but in every case peace was eventually made. The alien group was eventually incorporated, in the Catskill tradition, just as the Irish have made a place for themselves, the Dutch, the Scotch-Irish, the Hasidim, the French Huguenots, the Italians. Now the population of those who make their life around craft is a very diverse one, with a native-born quilter, eighty-nine years old, at one end of the spectrum, and a Haitian potter, resident for three years, at the other end.

Of course, craft has changed since the nineteenth century, and has become worthy of a definition. For the sake of this book, I have not defined it as folk art. Many of the craftspeople of the Catskills are trained at colleges and art schools. I define craft as the making of useful objects by hand, one at a time. For the most part, the craftspeople in this book use traditional methods, but obviously, the potters do not fire in brick ovens over wood fires, nor do the woodworkers scorn the use of machines per se. Just as the Catskills are part of the living landscape, the craftspeople live in our times, as subject as anyone to larger market forces, technology, and social change. Only one of the profiles that follow is of someone whose work does not adhere strictly to the above definition, and that is of Marcia Guthrie, who makes a kind of elaborate paper doll. I have included her work not only because it is beautiful and unique, and because the techniques are simple, homegrown ones, but also because her work grows out of a very traditional domestic occupation, that of entertaining children.

Why, in a world where everything can be bought, and all the necessities are available at a reasonable price, should so many people be making things? That lots of people are making things, and lots of their things are being bought, is indisputable. This year, at the Rhinebeck Crafts Fair, in Dutchess County, 350 exhibitors were chosen from a pool of over 1,000 applicants. At the American Crafts Council Fair, in West Springfield, Baltimore, and San Francisco, there were nearly 900 exhibitors or stand-by exhibitors. In addition to such general fairs as these, more specialized events must be factored in—miniature shows, for example, or wildlife expositions. And not every craftsman desires or needs these shows to sell his work—some have their own stores. Some sell through agents, others sell at private shows given by friends. Some sell by word of mouth or through advertising. Some take commissions.

In short, business is being done, and nearly everyone who has been in the business for any length of time remarks on how much more business is being done than there used to be, how much more sophisticated the business is, and how much more expensive the handcrafted objects have become.

There is, as a result of that interesting movement fifteen to twenty years ago back to art, craft, and nature, a sophisticated appreciation of American craft, and a market for well-made objects. Among the craftspeople there is a thriving interest in craft techniques—both in retaining old techniques and inventing new ones. An example would be the introduction of the principle of the pizza cutter to the world of quilting. The old, laborious process of cutting out fabric has been speeded up and made more accurate, and, simultaneously, new patterns that make interesting use of the strips and diamonds and squares most easily produced by the pizza cutter have joined more traditional ones in the quilter's repertoire. Another would be the use of casting and molds in "serious" pottery.

Although there aren't as many craftspeople as there are lawyers, stockbrokers, and doctors, the lives of one group comment on the lives of the other group in some intriguing ways.

The similarities and contrasts are especially apparent among those aged thirty-five to forty-five, and especially in the Catskills and New England, where the two groups not only come into contact with one another, but also share a good deal of background—middle class upbringing, college education. A number of craftspeople went from college into business before choosing the more economically perilous life of making things to sell. One similarity between the two groups is that they have both changed the worlds they entered fifteen years ago. Those who began living by craft brought an educated sense of design, a trained eye, and a sense of pride: Exposed to "art," but choosing "craft," they closed the gap between art and craft, in both style and price. Another similarity is that both groups brought a lot of energy and ambition to their careers, which may be the spur that has institutionalized the crafts fairs to such a degree. And the crafts fairs are full of only the best materials: pure wool sweaters, silk blouses, black walnut furniture, porcelain pots, pure cotton quilts, gold, and precious stones. If there's anything that the postwar generation likes, it is the sense of working with the best, and then owning the best.

The great difference between the craftspeople and many of their brothers and sisters in the city (literally, most of the craftspeople in this book do have brothers and sisters in the city) is that the craftspeople have chosen work over career. They have arranged their lives around those hours in the shop when they are at work making butter dishes or chairs, and for all of them, the primary motivation is the pleasure of making rather than the prospect of profit. Those who must maintain a certain level of repetitive production to fill orders seek ways to bring creativity to the details of their work and ways to shift production to others, through licensing their designs, so that they can work on something new. While they recognize the "cost" of creativity in lost production time, they are willing to endure the cost, and have chosen to live in an inexpensive way so that they can afford the cost. The result of this choice, for those craftspeople who are working in a medium that suits them, is a surprising lack of alienation. And where the craftsperson does feel alienated, he or she always locates it in the medium rather than in the style of life he or she has chosen. The fact is, those craftspeople who are working in a congenial medium seem enthusiastic and happy, whatever the other ups and downs of their lives. Obviously, the thirty-five craftspeople I interviewed for this book (including those not profiled) are a small sample, but it stands to reason that regular engagement with an activity that gives many kinds of pleasure forms a solid spiritual base for the rest of life. At any rate, none of the craftspeople I spoke to is intending to return to law school.

Every craftsperson I interviewed for this book saw his or her choice to live in the Catskills as being significantly entwined with his or her choice to live by craft. For some, it had been a matter of economics—cheaper to live here than in the city, for example—that became a matter of aesthetic preference. Almost everyone, when asked why he or she lived in the Catskills, answered with some version of, "But it's so beautiful here!" and everyone looked around in wonder. For a few, the craft itself is an expression of the natural life of the place. One spends time in the woods looking for likely natural forms that he can apply to his vases and dishes. For others, the decision to live in the Catskills predated the decision to live by craft, and then living by craft came to seem appropriate and possible after accepting the rhythms of Catskill life. For all of them, there is a connection—the beauty of the natural environment seems to express itself in the craftsman's urge to make something beautiful, or the craftsman's inborn aesthetic sense is satisfied by the surrounding beauty. Unlike their brothers and sisters in the city, these craftspeople must make few aesthetic compromises with their world.

It is 1986, and the men and women who follow are as up to date and present in the modern world as anyone else. They drive cars and own VCRs and get cable TV, though I don't think any of them happens to own a personal computer. What follows is not only a friendship quilt, but also a snapshot of a particular place at a particular time. I offer it with that photo album sort of affection, and with that photo album desire to save the passing moment for oneself and for others.

© Michael Owen

# John Hoeko

A Tensor light is angled low over the desk, and countless objects, ranging in size from small to tiny, are neatly laid out around the vise. The vise, thin, round-nosed, stands up from the edge of the desk, attached by a small C-clamp. To the left, brightly colored spools of nylon and silk thread stand in ranks. To the right, two or three small instruments, a pair of surgical scissors, a bobbin, and a pair of hackle pliers. John Hoeko, who spends most of his days operating a bulldozer, is about to tie a dry fly. Flies are for attracting the attention of trout (or, in other parts of the world, salmon, bass, bonefish). It is neither a bait nor a lure, but more like a calculated deception.

John is thirty-seven years old, a lifelong resident of the Catskills. He has been fly-fishing and fly tying for most of his life. Fly-fishing in American began not far from where he is sitting, about forty miles to the south, along the Beaverkill and the Neversink, around the turn of the century. He has blue eyes and dark, curly hair, and he is big, big across the chest and shoulders, big around the arms, big in the fingers. He takes out a gamecock neck and plucks a single feather from it. There used to be dry-fly purists with the leisure to breed their own roosters, whose feathers had just the proper stiffness and water-resistance for good dry flies, but there aren't so many of those anymore. This neck is from India. The shiny feathers vary in color from reddish tan to a deep russet. Other necks, for other flies, are other colors. There is a color, called blue dun, that is so rare as to be almost mythical. He takes a silver tool that he made from a surgical instrument and grasps the barbules about a third of the way down one side of the feather quill, then strips them off. He does this on the other side of the quill, then puts it to soak in a small glass of water.

Fixed in the vise is a bronze hook. Deeply imbedded hooks are occasionally left in the mouths of the fish, and the powerful digestive fluids of the fish can dissolve a bronze hook in a month or two. This hook is about half an inch long. Hanging from the vise is a spool of nylon thread. It looks like a gossamer filament until he holds some of the other threads up to the light. They might have been spun by spiders. John specializes in very small flies. The one he is making now is a rather large one and is of a type known as a ginger variant, which is intended to mimic a mayfly. He winds the nylon thread neatly around the shank of the hook so that the wraps lie side by side without overlapping. The bits of feather and thread will be attached to these wraps rather than to the bare hook. Now he takes a good pinch of the barbules that he stripped from the quill and he lays them along the hook, near the bend. He wraps the thread around them, and they form the tail, protruding beyond the bend of the hook about half an inch.

Next, he picks the stripped quill from the water and lays it along the shank of the hook, securing it with a few wraps of thread. The windings of the quill around the shank form the body of the fly. He goes back to the gamecock neck, seeking two more hackles. These two are rather smaller than the first one. He removes the barbules from one side of each, and, one at a time, he attaches each quill to the shank of the hook close to the eye. He winds the quill around the shank of the hook so that the barbules spread stiffly into a many spoked wheel around the axis of the hook. These hackles are meant to represent the wings and legs of the insect. They are tied down with thread and then secured with head cement, a sort of hard-drying lacquer.

After a few minutes the lacquer dries. John takes the fly out of the vise and sets it on the desk. The tips of the tail and the tips of the hackles lift the barb of the hook off the table, as, when the fly is used, they will lift it off the surface of the water. The fly is neatly balanced so that the bend of the hook is downward and the barb is pointing upward at an angle, ready to be taken into the fish's mouth and "set" by the fisherman, that is, hooked into the soft parts by a gentle lifting of the rod. Even so, John is dissatisfied with the fly. Two or three of the barbules forming the wing section angle outward, away from the others. It is not clear whether the fish will notice this and be put off his feed, or whether it is simply that John notices it.

There are other ways to catch fish. Bears use their paws. Commercial fishermen use nets. If you hang a piece of string in the water with a worm on a hook at the end of it, a fish might come along and get caught on the hook while trying to take the worm. But dry-fly fishermen are driven not by a need to have fish—much of their catch they measure and throw back—but by an aesthetic need. The scope of this aesthetic can be judged by the number of books that have been written on the subject of fly-fishing, thousands for every book on any other sort of fishing, and by the meditative tone of much of the literature. Roderick Haig-Brown, chancellor of the University of Victoria and a judge of the Provincial Court of British Columbia, wrote many books on fly-fishing. Before he died in 1976, he wrote the following:

> If the fish is to be risen and securely hooked, the deception must be total. The fly must be placed precisely from an angle and a distance that conceal the fisherman and his movements. The fly must be the right one or some deliberately chosen variation from it. The float must be perfect, a drift with the current as natural as though the fly were unattached. The fish must rise and take the fly in complete faith. The fisherman's response must be exactly timed, firm enough to set the hook and smooth enough to avoid any risk of breaking the leader.

This sort of purism was a British import—dry fly-fishing originated in the 1840s in southern England on chalk streams such as the Itchen and the Test, and was common there by the 1850s. Although some experts disagree, the acknowledged father of American dry fly-fishing, that is, the first man to import dry flies from England and use them in American streams, is said to have been Theodore Gordon, a New Yorker who, because of illness, had retired from the banks of Wall Street to the banks of the Beaverkill. He is known to have written to Frederic Halford, a famous British flytier, inquiring about dry fly-fishing, and to have received in return a selection of Halford's flies. Gordon seems to have been the first American to use flies that were tied to float on the water and resist wetting—previous fishermen and authors advised using false casts to whip the fly though the air, drying it. Gordon also invented a number of flies that specifically imitated native insects, such as the mayfly and the caddis fly, in various stages of development. The history of fly-fishing and fly-tying in the three generations since Gordon is closely linked to Catskill streams—numerous writers and fly inventors, such as Edward Hewitt, Preston Jennings, Art Flick, Harry and Elsie Darbee, and Walt and Winnie Dette, grew up or made their homes not far from the Beaverkill and the Willowemoc.

John Hoeko is profoundly aware of the heritage, and his place in it, in the fourth generation. He ties his flies in the Catskill style—drably colored and "sparsely dressed." He also ties flies small enough to imi-

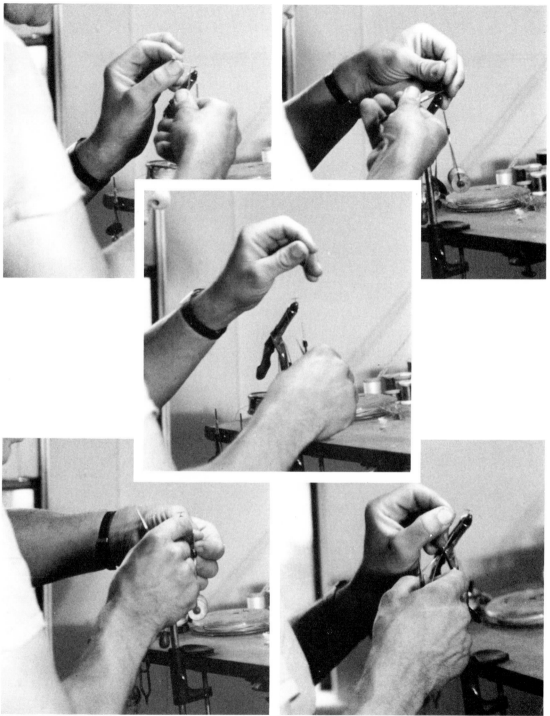

tate midges and "terrestrials," a special group of flies that mimic land insects that have fallen into the stream by accident. It is for this reason that he is dissatisfied with his ginger variant. It might catch a fish, but catching a fish is not entirely the point.

Fishing is good on the Beaverkill, even in 1986. Catskill streams, according to John, are about as clean as they were in his childhood, thirty years ago, and that is still clean enough to afford a confident drink, still clean enough for crystal clarity in most places. The Esopus and the two branches of the Neversink rise on the flanks of Slide Mountain. The Beaverkill runs down the west side of Doubletop. They are country streams, far enough into the woods to escape contamination by towns, and even by farms. They support three types of trout: native brook, rainbow, and a large population of hardier, gamier, and more interesting, but nonetheless imported (from Germany and Scotland) brown trout. The brown trout are actually of a different genus from the brook trout and the rainbow, more closely related to salmon.

Fishing is good on the Beaverkill not because it is easy to catch fish there, but because it isn't, even though the stream is full of fish. Fly fishermen apparently prefer a worthy opponent, and the fish of the Beaverkill are wily and sophisticated, reducing an expert fisherman, as the story is told of Art Flick, to crawling toward the stream so that the fish won't see him coming. Do fish think? Do fish learn? John laughs. "Sometimes I think they're smarter than people. When I figure out the mystery . . ." His voice trails off in full confidence that he never will.

Fishing is also good elsewhere in the Catskills, on the Schoharie, on both branches of the Delaware, on the Esopus, and on the smallest streams, too. Though the Esopus is one of the region's most famous streams, and some people say that they only fish the Delaware when the Esopus is too crowded, John prefers the Delaware drainage system. On various outings on the Esopus, he has broken two bamboo rods (expensive), and had a number of falls. "I can't do anything right on the stream," he says. Where is his favorite spot? He laughs self-deprecatingly, but he isn't saying. Somewhere. He begins to tie another fly. What is hard about it? "Nothing," he says. On a good day, he can tie twelve an hour. He will take three or four boxes of flies with him to the stream on any given day, countless psychological tests for trout—tests for taste and mood and sensitivity and alertness, a deception, not a bait.

They seem extreme, these two things that he does, excavating with a bulldozer and tying flies, and at rest, he looks more like a bulldozer operator than anything else, but his large hands move with firm, sinuous delicacy, manipulating small tools and smaller materials with confidence and accuracy. The fact is that both are in his blood, as he says. His father was a fisherman, his uncle taught him how to tie flies. His father worked as an excavator. He defends the bulldozer at some length: "It's a machine and the effects are of enormous magnitude, what it does to the environment. Most people aren't aware of that. I feel I'm aware of that. I also feel that it allows you to do some wonderful things as well as mess something up. It depends on what use it's put to. For instance, I like to do stream restoration work, to stabilize an eroding bank, for example, though to get permits and this and that is very complicated. That sort of thing used to be done back in the thirties, with the WPA and so forth." As on the lower Mississippi? No. "Flood control is a double-edged sword, because it can destroy a river in the guise of ameliorating flood problems for land owners. For example, there's stream channelization, where it's basically that they carve out the stream—that increases the velocity of the water. It's going to do more damage down below, so you go back the next year and do it again. It never ends. I basically believe in leaving the stream as is, but if there's some man-made damage, then you can go in there and rectify it in some way, in most cases, and one tool you can do it with is a bulldozer." His usually soft voice has risen. The issue isn't an idle one with him.

Twelve or thirteen years ago, John was the primary lobbyist for a group known as Catskill Waters. Educated partly at Columbia University, and partly at the University of Denver Business School, he returned to the Catskills after five years in Colorado and was invited into Catskill Waters by a Woodstock friend, Fred Mele. The fight was against City Hall—New York City Hall. The history of the battle was a rather long one. In 1931, the U.S. Supreme Court granted the City of New York the right to divert water from the Delaware drainage system to its own use. A case could be made that the city, having fouled its own natural water source, the Hudson River, was allowed by the Supreme Court to steal water from its neighbors. At any rate, the city, by eminent domain, condemned land and built six reservoirs in the Catskills: the Rondout, the Neversink, and the Schoharie, on streams of the same names; the Ashokan, on the Esopus; the Cannonsville, on the West Branch of the Delaware; and last, the Pepacton, below Margaretville on the East Branch of the Delaware. John remembers the construction of

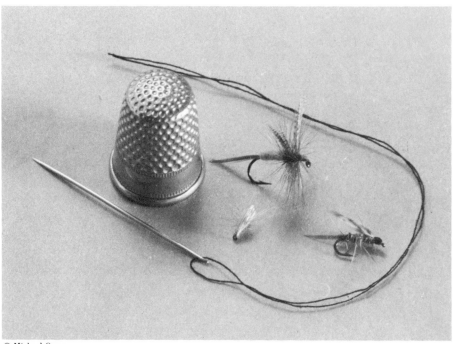

© Michael Owen

the Pepacton, which was begun in the early fifties: "I remember when I was a kid, traveling along Thirty down there and watching houses being pushed into heaps and burnt up. It was apocalyptic." These waters are owned by the City of New York, and signs all around each reservoir assert this fact. The issues surrounding the reservoirs are complex, perhaps troubling, but also moot, since the reservoirs are built, and the amount of discharge on the Delaware drainage is controlled outside of the region by the rivermaster down in New Jersey.

One issue, however, was not moot thirteen years ago, and that was the system of releasing water from the various reservoirs. John is blunt. "The worst problem in the Catskills is how New York City operates the reservoirs, which affects downstream releases, which affect the rivers. The city was dumping out of one reservoir, the Cannonsville, over and over, and releasing virtually nothing from the East Branch." The results were disastrous—the entire stream below the impoundment at Downsville threatened to become a series of stagnant, hot pools, with water temperatures as high as 90 degrees, which in turn produced massive fish kills. The final solution was passage of the Water Release Bill, which forces the New York City Environmental Protection Agency to account for water releases, and to consult the needs of the stream systems as well as the needs of city bureaucracy in determining reservoir use. Catskill Waters did not begin with legislative remedies, but New York City agencies were unresponsive to other forms of persuasion. "They would just say unequivocally, unilaterally, 'No!' Just no to anything upstate. I went down to one of my first meetings after I was made president of this group, Catskill Waters, and I sat with this guy who was commissioner of water resources, which determined all the reservoirs, and I asked him, 'If we could demonstrate to you that our water release proposal would not adversely affect your water supply by a drop, would you implement it?' and he said, 'Young man, you know, when I was your age, Franklin Delano Roosevelt told me never to answer a hypothetical question.' I saw red! I started to leap up from the table!" He laughs, "I was young, you know. I didn't care!" He laughs again.

The bill had no trouble in the Senate—"It went through the Senate on greased skids," John says, because upstate senators are always kindly toward a bill that might inconvenience the folks downstate, but the Assembly was controlled, of course, by the city. He was in Albany off and on during all of 1975, then constantly throughout 1976. Methods? He laughs again. "I never disappeared. I was there constantly. They had to eat, breathe, and drink me every day. I was like a piece of gum on the bottom of their shoe. I just never let go." The experience, even though a victorious one, didn't leave him with a taste for further victories, or respect for the incorruptability of Albany politicians. "Sophisticated" is how he terms them. The bill passed ten years ago. John has been excavating and fly-fishing ever since, though he occasionally gives an interview or a talk about the issue.

He takes another fly out of the vise and rocks it back and forth on the palm of his hand. It is a hair-winged royal coachman. He says, "I haven't been fishing enough lately. I used to go a lot." What is a lot? Every day? Lately he goes about once a week, maybe twice. A few years ago he did often go every day. He pauses, rocking the fly back and forth, then says, "There's something about moving water that draws me. The interplay of it with rocks and vegetation and trees. It's like a universal constant for me. It's stabilizing and reassuring, and cements me to this planet." What about fishing? "That light, well-crafted bamboo pole and that line form a deep spiritual connection as well as a physical one. It's also a barometer of my feelings and moods. What I am feeling is reflected back to me immediately." He sets the fly with the other one. Lots of times he catches fish, too.

# Rhea Silber

**O**nce," says Rhea Silber, "I fell off my chair spinning. I was sitting right here by the fire, and it was warm, and the radio was on, you know, and the next thing I knew I was falling asleep and nearly out of my chair." Rhea has eight spinning wheels, soon to be nine, but you don't need a spinning wheel to spin. All you really need is some carded wool and a twirling, heavy object, known as a drop spindle. The principle, like most handcraft principles, is a simple one, and Rhea demonstrates it. Her drop spindle looks rather like a child's top, with a shaft about a foot long that runs through a thick disk some 4 inches in diameter. The point of the shaft sticks out below the disk. Wound around the shaft just above the disk is wool thread, and this thread ends in a tuft of unspun wool called a *rolag*. Rhea raises her arms. In the fingers of her left hand, she holds the thread just where it unwinds into the rolag. With her right, she gives the drop spindle a quick twist, and it begins twirling toward the floor. As it turns, she uses her right hand to pull the twisting thread out of the rolag, monitoring the tension a little as she talks. When the spool hits the floor, she picks it up and winds the newly spun thread onto it. The spinning wheel was invented around 1500, though experts disagree about the exact date. The drop spindle is probably as old as human civilization.

Rhea likes this ancient method of spinning because it so clearly shows the principles that work to make thread out of fiber. The fiber can be any sort of animal hair—Rhea raises Angora goats, which produce mohair. She has also spun with the hair from Angora rabbits, which produce angora, and the hair from dogs (collie hair has the reputation for producing very soft fabric). She has spun silk and flax (for linen). But her favorite and the favorite of most hand spinners is wool. The history and culture of hand spinning are closely linked to the population distribution of sheep. Athena, for instance, was the Greek goddess of both wisdom and spinning, and the hills of Greece were and still are largely given over to sheep and goat raising. Sheep and goats can live on more marginal lands than those needed to support cattle, and they also are more totally useful than cattle, since they produce wool as well as milk, meat, and skins. The useful life of a sheep begins almost immediately—lambs may be slaughtered for meat, or sheared for lambswool. At a year, a ewe may be bred, milked, sheared. Ewes have little trouble giving birth, but need a fair amount of preventive care—worming three or four times a year, foot trimming, dipping for parasites.

The production of wool cloth from sheep's fleece is time-consuming, and for centuries engaged a significant percentage of family effort. Most sheep are sheared in the winter, before lambing, and after a year of grazing in the fields. Rhea's fleeces are always clean, because the animals are kept in clean pastures all summer, and winter on clean bedding. After shearing, the wool is picked by hand, to remove whatever dirt is there, and to separate the fibers. Then it is carded. The two cards look like poodle brushes. Rhea places a hank of clean wool on one of them and rubs them briskly across one another, pulling outward, then lifting them apart and repeating the motion. After about a minute, she separates the cards to reveal a puff of wool about the size and shape of a very airy bratwurst. This is the rolag. The wool fibers have been teased into one direction, around the diameter of the rolag. Next, this rolag will literally be "spun"—all the fibers will be twisted more or less tightly together in a continuous thread. The technical name for thread spun from rolags is *yarn*, as in woolen yarn. The combed fleece can, however, be carded into *bats* rather than rolags. These are longer—flat, loose, feltlike strips of wool about the width of adding machine paper, some 14 inches long, which Rhea makes herself on a mechanical carding machine that her son electrified for her. In these bats, the fibers run lengthwise, and the yarn they produce is called *worsted* as in summer-weight worsted. Worsted thread is smoother and more uniform than yarn, because of the direction the fibers run.

Spinning itself is easier to demonstrate than to describe, since the goal is a smooth and continuous thread and the expertise is in coordination of hands (holding rolag and thread), feet (turning the wheel), and touch (perceiving the appropriate tension that will cause the thread to twist to the proper tightness but not cause it to break). For beginners, says Rhea, who has taught numerous people to spin, the greatest frustration is repeatedly breaking the thread, which is why she likes to start people on the drop spindle, because it can be more easily controlled than the spinning wheel.

The spinning wheel is actually a foot-driven engine that works on what you might call the fan-belt principle. The most obvious element of the machine, the large wheel, serves only to turn the bobbin and spindle, which twist the thread. The axle of the wheel is attached by a primitive drive shaft to the treadle. Rhea pumps the treadle with her

foot, the wheel turns, moving the drive band (the fan belt) around the smaller wheel attached to the bobbin. With her right hand, Rhea holds the rolag about 8 inches from the bobbin, and with her left, she monitors the tension of the thread, which travels through a small eye as it's twisted, then winds itself onto the bobbin. Spinning on the wheel eliminates one step, twirling the whorl by hand, and consolidates the other two—twisting the thread and winding it on the bobbin. Obviously, spinning with the wheel is considerably faster than spinning with the drop spindle, but it still takes Rhea a long time to spin enough yarn for a sweater. Rhea does not spin for a living.

At fifty-two, Rhea has the energy, and the wiry athleticism, of a woman half her age. By nine in the morning, she has already fed the livestock and been to Bovina Center on the back of her friend Ralph's Honda 1200 motorcycle to deliver blueberry muffins to the boys gathered around the gas station for the Saturday morning gossip. Ralph is a native—he was raised on a dairy farm near Shavertown, which is now at the bottom of the Pepacton Reservoir. Rhea moved to the Catskills from New Jersey twenty-two years ago. They have been friends for two years now, but they still look at each other quizzically across the kitchen table. Ralph sold his dairy farm some years ago, when it was still profitable, and seems pleased to follow a lifetime of livestock and the labor they demand with another lifetime of leisure. He is at home with Rhea's animals (forty sheep, six goats, four horses, three dogs, and countless cats).

Now Rhea pulls a chair up to the table and puts down her cup of coffee. They look at each other and laugh. The trip to Bovina Center, population about 150, was a favor to Rhea's neighbor, who had to be away when it was his turn to supply the muffins. Ralph and Rhea were glad to do it. That they were a rather scandalous sight, however, puts them in an especially good mood. Also at the table are two dolls in highchairs, Adam and Zachary. The dolls are Rhea's, part of a large collection. There seem to be large collections of everything: mottoes on the bulletin board, orchids in the greenhouse, spinning wheels, teddy bears. A new puppy, a Yorkshire terrier about as big as a blueberry muffin, weighing in at a pound and a half, yelps and plays with the adult Yorkshire under the table. Hanging in the doorway to the dining room are skeins of wool sheared from Rhea's sheep, carded, combed, and spun by Rhea on one of the eight spinning wheels. They are dyed blue with Tintex "or something" she says, but she usually uses natural dyes from weeds, bark, nuts, onion skins, lichens. Her dark eyes sparkle. Her favorite motto is "I may be getting older but I'll never grow up."

Rhea and her husband, Harold, who died in 1981, moved to the Catskills on impulse. He was a dentist in New Jersey who had spent some time hunting woodchucks around Bovina on the weekends. They bought the farm she owns now and came up during the summers for four years. In spite of the fact that he was born and raised in Newark and she was born and raised in suburban New Jersey, there was no period of adjustment. Their amusements had already diverged from those of their friends in New Jersey: "One day I was at a party, and someone turned to me and said, 'Rhea, you haven't said anything. What's the matter?' I said, 'Well, all you're talking about is where to go in Europe and restaurants and shows and things. If you'd like to talk about shoeing a horse or shearing sheep, I'd be glad to do that.' That's when I knew, I think." She has never missed it. "I never went back," she says. "I never even went back to pack." One Sunday at the end of August, twenty-two years ago, they made up their minds to stay. The next day, Rhea enrolled their three sons in school, and Harold went back to New Jersey and sold the house. "We didn't tell anyone, not our parents or relatives or friends."

Impulse got them into the sheep-raising business, too. "My husband said, 'If you're going to spin, we might as well have a sheep.' So we went to buy a sheep. Then we decided one sheep would get lonely, so then you had to have two sheep. But then he said, 'Gee, but you know, if we're going to have two sheep then we might as well have a lamb.' So we came home with three sheep, and before I knew it we had sixty sheep." They didn't start with Corriedales, the breed she now specializes in, a New Zealand breed valuable for their meat and their long, fine, wool, and in fact tried about seven breeds before deciding on the Corriedales. They are not pets, and she feels no hesitation about having them slaughtered. Of the forty sheep now in the pasture, only twenty will find themselves in the barn in the winter.

They built the barn, renovated the house, rode horses, and sheared sheep. Harold named the six-year-old mastiff Athena. They built horse stalls together, picked blackberries, made jam, raised three sons, now thirty-two, thirty, and twenty-two. It was the sort of marriage that is a phenomenon—when they met, he was seventeen, she was thirteen. "He was a big shot," she says with a chuckle. "He already drove and everything." The scene of their meeting set the tone for the rest of their lives—it was at her aunt's summer cabin on Lake Musconetcong, New Jersey, where his parents also had a cabin. They went fishing, hiking, camping, and picnicking. They always made things together—"Before we got married we made all our own dishes." Later, the children were included. They had to have five horses, for instance, so that they could ride together. In the living room, Rhea picks up an antique skein winder, or reel, called a niddy-noddy. It is about 14 inches long, a sort of triangle with a spool at each point and two spools, offset from one another, at the apex. The yarn winds in a continuous circuit around all four spools. The boys used to wind the yarn and sing a song, "Niddy-noddy, niddy-noddy, two heads in one body." The "heads" are the dowels that take up the yarn, the body is the framework that holds them. Of her sons' lives she says, "There was always something to do. My boys never even went out on dates until they were seniors in high school. I always knew where they were."

A few minutes later, she is skipping over the 8 × 10 plank that is the bridge over the stream that runs below the pasture. She calls out apolo-

gies for the mud, then climbs over the gate and begins banging with a scoop on a bucket of sheep feed, and calling, "Hey sheep! Hey sheep!" They appear, bells clanging around their necks, and approach readily, somewhat to Rhea's surprise. They even approach me, though they don't know me. Sheep are normally shy. "They're moronic," says Rhea, possibly the reason she dismisses the idea of hesitating to slaughter, or eat, them. Ralph remarks that a successful farmer can't get attached to the livestock. The farm buildings sit in a kind of bowl, and around them rise a hundred acres of fields and woods, intensely green, though the lighter, opener green of the western Catskill farmland rather than the deep, black-green of eastern Catskill forests. The sky is about as intensely blue as a sky could be. The horses appear, shyer, or not as hungry. They approach much more reluctantly, a palomino that is obviously elderly, maybe twenty-five, and her son, a large chestnut. When they come into the group of sheep, the sheep turn in a panic and run off. One of the sheep falls under the others and is stepped on, but she is soon on her feet and racing away.

After Harold died, Rhea had the farm on the market for two years, unable to bear living where she had been so happy. She says, "I just have never seen another place I like better, except New Zealand." Ralph speaks up. "She's going to have to hunt a long time before she finds a place—"

"He's from the area, from a hundred years ago. He's a hundred years old. So he's prejudiced."

He says, "I always thought farming was a great life."

Finally, Rhea couldn't leave. There is the sense in the house, and around the farm, that it would be impossible to pack everything up. It would certainly be difficult to pack up the *other* house, a dollhouse made by her son Martin, a replica of a plantation house in Louisiana, that he began to work on when he was a junior in high school. The floor in each room is of a different material. The library floor, for example, is black walnut. The entryway floor is parquet, blond and dark.

The floor of the dining room is black and white marble, each square individually cut. The staircase curves upward, the newel post intricately carved. The rugs are needlepoint, the furniture, some of which Martin made and some of which they bought, is all to scale (1 inch to 1 foot), which means that the thickness of the desktop on the secretary in the library is about that of a sheet of paper. It is made of mahogany, however. It has not one but two secret compartments. The roof dormers come complete with flashing, the shutters and shingles are handmade. There are chairs on the front veranda, two carriages with horses between the shafts on the front driveway.

And it would be difficult to pack up the looms. A loom is rather a large piece of furniture that was common in every working household until the advent of water- and steam-driven looms in the great mills of the early modern era. The rule of thumb is that it takes seven carders to keep one spinner spinning, and seven spinners to keep one weaver weaving, but hand weaving is painstaking and time-consuming, too. The threads of the warp have to be carefully tied to the warp beam in the back and the cloth beam in the front. A tightly woven wool fabric of a simple pattern could easily have twenty threads per inch, which, for a 44-inch-wide piece of weaving, would be 1,760 separate knots. The number of times the weaver will then have to throw the shuttle back and forth between the two sides, or selvages, would depend on the projected length of the fabric. Four yards? 2,880 individual throws. The intricacy of the weaving, of course, varies widely, depending on the fineness of the fiber. There can be as few as two or three throws, or *picks*, per inch, or as many as forty. Weaving was one of the earliest crafts to be mechanized, and even, it might be said, computerized. As early as the eighteenth century, in water-powered French mills, the multicolored and intricately figured patterns of jacquard weaving were punched onto cards and run through the looms on drums not unlike the drums that run player pianos.

Such jacquard looms are much more complex than Rhea's largest, which is set up in a sun porch off her bedroom, overlooking the barn. The red and white drapes on the windows are woven in a starlike "winter-and-summer" pattern she calls *overshot*. Rhea and Harold designed and wove the fabric, then made the drapes. A yellow coverlet in the guest room is another piece they designed and executed. Harold especially enjoyed working out the mathematics of complicated weaves —hanging from the door is a blue and white houndstooth jacket he wove, and in the closet is a yellow plaid skirt and vest. Much of the thread in every piece was sheared from their own sheep, picked, carded, spun, dyed, woven, and sewn into clothing or drapes, though, because weaving is quicker than spinning and carding, some was purchased.

Rhea feels both at home and not at home in the Catskills. Down the road is a new house, built within sight of the breakfast table, on a piece of land that the owner sold for less than Rhea and Harold offered to pay for it. It used to be that Rhea would look out at that house over her breakfast coffee and cry at the sight. Then she moved the table slightly so that she couldn't see it. At first she says that the neighbors didn't like her. Later she admits that anti-Semitism was a factor in the woman's refusal to sell. This, after all, is Bovina Center, not Liberty, not the Jewish Catskills. Mostly, however, she has been able to go her own way and to make friends. More than anything, people seem rather interested in what she is doing, although they are not likely to ask about it. She says, still amazed, "People will come by and just park the car and look. I had some girls come on a motorcycle one time and just wander around the house. I said, 'What are you doing here? We're having supper!' They said, 'We're patients of Dr. Silber, and we wanted to come and look at your place.' I said, 'Call me up and I'd be glad to make an appointment. Right now we're having supper.'"

They joke a bit about her "getting out from under all this," but she denies that, apart from the year or two following her husband's death, all the animals and activities and responsibilities have ever seemed like too much for her. She is up at six, goes to bed toward midnight. When Harold was in practice, he would do the chores before he went off to work, then change his clothes after a day in the office and they would work until dark. They added on the greenhouse and Harold started to grow orchids. He learned about natural dyeing and gave dyeing workshops when she gave spinning and weaving demonstrations. She used to take her spinning wheel and spin in the front seat of their truck when they went on trips.

Rhea pulls out one bed coverlet that she is especially fond of. It is huge, knitted, the lacey pattern taken from a nineteenth-century original. There is one like it over the bed of the child's room at the Frisbee House, a historical restoration outside of Delhi. The white wool she sheared off her own sheep, then spun. She talks about the pattern, how authentic it is. Harold loved it, she says. The pieces were so small she used to take it everywhere, a leaf pattern that fit together, triangles into squares, squares into strips, strips into bedspread. She would take the knitting with her when she took Harold to the hospital for his chemotherapy treatments, which would last two hours. It is huge. After I admire it, she looks at it for a few moments, then we fold it up. She keeps it in the living room, and she handles it with that weighty combination of ruefulness and love that has entered her whole life as the single remaining inhabitant of the world they, literally, built together with their own hands.

© Michael Owen

# Michael Boyer

**M**ichael Boyer's studio used to be a laundry. He has two rooms. The ceilings are high, the furnishings rough, and walls painted white. In the afternoon, the east windows afford a restful, bluish light. On racks against the walls, wide porcelain bowls are drying, another shade of white. In front of the wheel, the plaster wedging table is yet another shade of white. As he sits behind the wheel, he says, "Porcelain is the most pure form of clay. That's really the only difference between stoneware and porcelain, or any clay and porcelain. It has the least amount of impurities in it, and because of that it fires white, and becomes translucent if fired high enough. This clay is fired to cone ten, which is about twenty-four hundred degrees Fahrenheit. These bowls will be translucent if they're thin enough. I generally throw fairly thinly, so parts of them will be translucent."

His hands are slender, the fingers long. He centers the clay on the wheel with casual expertise—he has been making pots for fifteen years, since he was an undergraduate at Queens College, and has been teaching pottery for nearly that long. He quickly works the mound into a wide, squat cylinder and begins to press down upon it, first with the side of his hand, then with the fingers. His hands work together without hesitation, changing position continually, with such delicacy that they might only be feeling the clay, but are in fact shaping it. He says, "What you have to do is surround the clay with equal pressure, and control the pressure in your hands. Probably the most important thing is to increase and decrease the pressure gradually, because if I release my pressure quickly, the clay just spins out of shape, because it's a soft, malleable material." It is almost a magic trick—his hands move over the clay and a bowl takes shape. The visible exertion is more in his legs, stretched forward; his back and shoulders, curved over the wheel; and his forearms, which are braced against his thighs. He flattens out the base of the bowl and begins to bring up the sides, and remarks, "To me the most important thing in making a pot is the exterior surface, the continuity of the line. I like to have a real smooth line. And then I put texture on the bottom, which may sound contradictory, to smooth it out then to put texture on it, but if your basic line is really clean then any texture on it gives the pot a refinement."

He is dissatisfied with how he has expressed himself, but the effect is apparent in the bottoms of the bowls that are drying on the racks. A spiral that he has put there with his finger looks precise and pleasing, giving the shallow bowl depth and interest.

He says, "On a bowl, I spend most of the time on the inside, because that's the finished surface. The outside can always be trimmed to match the inside. It's true to a large extent on any pot, even a very closed one. When you make a pot you should think of the inside containment, not the wall of the pot itself."

Quickly, after only about five minutes, he is finishing the bowl, smoothing the rim with a piece of dry-cleaner plastic. He stops the wheel and takes off the bat—the pie-shaped platform he set the clay on and then set upon the wheel head. In two days, when the bowl dries to a leatherlike hardness, he will turn it upside down on the wheel and trim the bottom with a modeling tool. After that, when it has thoroughly dried, he will fire it the first time, the bisque firing, and this firing, at about 185 degrees, will produce the chemical reactions that transform it from clay to pottery. A piece of clay, no matter how hard, how thoroughly baked by the sun, let's say, can always be crushed, mixed with water, and formed into another shape. A piece of pottery cannot.

This is the fifth and last bowl of the morning. After setting it on the drying rack, he takes another lump of white clay from a bag next to the wedging table. He smiles. "This is my good stock." But he is disappointed in the consistency of the clay, it is too soft. He divides the clay into two pieces and spreads one of them on the plaster wedging surface, so that the clay will give up some of its moisture to the plaster. The other he begins to wedge, that is, to mix by hand. The motion is rather like the motion of kneading bread. With both hands, he pulls the top of the piece toward him, then pushes it downward. After a few moments, it begins to look a bit like a primitive ram's head. Has he ever been tempted to make more sculpturelike pieces, pieces with less function? His "no" is flat and definite. "I'm very functionally oriented," he says. Then, still working over the clay, he says, "One of the key elements to throwing is wedging the clay enough. A lot of my students try to take short cuts and generally run into trouble. The clay isn't thoroughly blended, which is more important than removing air bubbles. It's tiring, which is why they don't want to do it. You can buy it de-aired, but you still should wedge it, because even in the bag there's some evaporation, and the outside of the lump is a little bit harder than the inside. You have to really blend it together." He pushes it in from the sides, down against the table and away, so the clay spirals around the center.

Air bubbles break at the bottom. He counts, a hundred wedges. It takes about five minutes.

He sets the lump on a bat. "This shape is a kind of globe shape. I've had a lot of problems with it, so I leave them on the bat. But then the tops tends to crack, so I've learned that as soon as they release themselves from the bat, if I turn them over, then the top doesn't crack." He sets the bat on the wheel head. The clay is very white. He presses his foot on the pedal and the wheel begins to turn. "Most people cone up the clay when they center—they bring their hands up and flatten it

out—but that just softens the clay because it exposes more clay to water, so I don't do that. If the clay gets too soft, if it doesn't have strength, and if you're fighting the softness of the clay all the time, then your shape doesn't look as spontaneous. It looks more like a sagging balloon than something with bones in it."

He opens out the lump with the middle finger of his left hand, then the other fingers. Rapidly, the cylinder gains height, until it stands about ten inches. The diameter is maybe five inches. He maintains this cylindrical shape for a long minute, then puts the fingers of his left hand inside it. Suddenly a bulge begins to rise from the bottom to the top, and then disappears. He says, "I'm thinning the clay and shaping it at the same time, because if you just keep it cylindrical and then start swelling it out, it tends to throw off center. Once I have a basic round-ness, I can just refine it." It begins to bulge again, only this time the bulge is larger. Soon, the entire wall of the pot is bulging outward, and only a small neck at the top is the same diameter as the former cylinder.

He is dissatisfied. "Here's the problem with soft clay. It starts caving in." An indentation has appeared at the top of the bulge. Carefully, Michael puts the fingers of his left hand into the mouth of the jar. The indentation remains the same. He smiles. "This one may not survive," he says. A moment later, the indentation disappears, and the line be-tween the neck and the widest part of the bulge is smooth again.

He is concentrating, but not so much that he can't talk about how he glazes and what he intends to do with this pot, which is to spray it with overlapping glazes. Usually he follows another method that he has de-vised to achieve a very thin coating on all surfaces: First, he waxes the bottom of the pot and attaches a piece of clay to it, then he pours glaze inside the pot and pours it out again. Finally, using the attached piece of clay as a handle, he dips the pot into the glaze. Air trapped inside the upside down pot as he dips it prevents glaze from flowing over the glaze already on the inside of the pot. He never paints the glaze on. Now, he begins to close the neck inward with his thumbs and long middle fingers. First, the neck flares, then shrinks inward. He sticks the middle finger of his left hand into the opening, and eases the wall of the neck outward. In a moment, all signs of a neck have disappeared, and the line of the jar is perfectly rounded and continuous.

He is still dissatisfied with the consistency of the clay, though. He looks at it critically, and says, "There's a little negative line here, and a little indentation over there. If you look at the space around the piece rather than the surface of the pot, it's easier to see that. See, there's a low point right there, which I'd like to get out. If you look at the piece, you don't always see it." His head is very low and close to the pot, horizontal rather than vertical. "Now this top I want to flatten a little more, because the top opens out in the drying and the firing. Clay

© Michael Owen

changes its shape. It's very subtle. In a normal, more cylindrical piece, the tops always close some, so I always flare them out just a trifle more than I want them to be when they're done." A moment later: "I like to have a sense of volume in the piece. If you get a continuous line, it looks more like it's holding something."

Is there a point when he decides that the clay won't take any more shaping? He is a perfectionist. He says, "Yes. And I either throw it away or settle, if it's not too bad." He sits up and prepares to trim the outside, to refine and give more of a curve to the shape. "Now this trimming will either make or break the piece. I want to take enough off so that it isn't too heavy, but if I take too much off, it collapses." With other pieces, he lets the clay dry a day or so before trimming. "But if I

© Michael Owen

trim it now, that eliminates trimming when it's leather hard, and that eliminates a whole step." He points with the modeling tool to the bottom of the pot. The diameter of the bottom of the inside, which dictates how much he can trim off the outside without breaking through the wall of the pot, can't be tested with fingers—the pot is too tall and the opening is too narrow. He looks at it for a second, then begins to slice clay off the outer wall of the pot, from about the widest part of the shape downward. He trims it smaller and smaller around the bottom, working carefully and pausing before the cuts, to give it a more voluminous shape and to compensate for the thickness added by the downward flow of the glaze that will come later. Soon the bottom looks impossibly small, giving the pot a cloudlike fullness.

Does he ever wish he had gone into something else? He smiles. "All the time." What does he fantasize having gone into? "Design. I think I would make a good designer. And also, pottery's a lot of hard work." He is almost finished. He says, "This shape takes a long time." He has been working for about twenty minutes. He has finished trimming, graduating the clay a bit, so that he won't leave a ridge where the trimmed part meets the untrimmed part. Now for the last step. "I make a little indentation at the very bottom like this. The glaze will end at the upper edge of it, but the indentation gives it lift off the table, so that it doesn't look like it's attached to the table. It creates a little shadow line that separates it from whatever it's sitting on."

He undercuts the edge with a pin, to help it separate from the bat as it dries, and to prevent the bottom from cracking. He lifts the bat off the wheel. He first started making this shape about six years ago, and has made quite a few of them—as many as forty in a series. The glazes "do wonderful things" on the shape, breaking and flowing over the curves.

Unlike most potters, Michael prefers glazing to making the pots, and in fact, for all that he considers himself a "functionally oriented person," he likes the pots he makes more as shapes for working out glazes

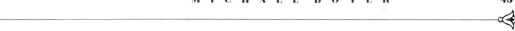

than as functional objects. Many potters test glazes, seeking the right predictable combination for producing a long series of saleable wares, but when the testing is over they are relieved. Michael, however, tests glazes the way mathematicians do proofs—just to see what will come out. Once he made 144 mugs, all the same size and shape, and glazed them with variations of the same glaze. What did he do after he was finished with that series? Go into production? "I stopped making those, because I'd learned what I wanted to know about the glaze." Did he then file that information for future use? "Well, not really. When you start using a glaze again, you have to test it out again and practice with it."

Glaze chemistry is very complex, especially if the potter is working with a gas-fired kiln, where the quantity of oxygen inside the chamber holding the pots is reduced in the course of the firing. Carbon monoxide is produced by the burning of the fuel, and this unstable gas reacts with oxygen in the glazes. A single glaze is a mix of silica with various chemicals called *fluxes*. The chemical reactions between the fluxes, between the fluxes and the silica, between the glaze and the clay of the pot, and between the atmosphere of the kiln and the glazes and the clay determine the color of the final pot. The temperature changes in the kiln and the hottest temperature the kiln reaches, as well as temperature variations around the chamber, also affect results. With an electric kiln, where the amount of oxygen remains constant, results are relatively more predictable, but every ceramist must resign himself to the possibility of a piece being ruined in the kiln.

In the front room, he has set out about twelve pots of various shapes and sizes on a table, the part of his collection that he keeps in Pine Hill. A tea pot, a mug, a small ginger jar, some others. How often does he fire his kiln? "About six times a year." How often is he satisfied with most or all of the pots in the kiln? "You mean, how often do I open the kiln and not say, 'Yuck'? Maybe twice a year." He picks up a blue ginger jar. Around the top rim, the blue glaze has broken up and turned bright white in the kiln. He holds it and looks at it with pleasure. It is a beautiful pot—perfectly shaped, to the average eye, a rich, bright blue with lots of depth. The white speckling draws the eye to the curve. It is elegant, but subtle. In a row of larger, brighter, more stylized pots, it could be overlooked. The lines are classical rather than avant-garde. He sets it down. He isn't often satisfied. He says, "In fifteen years of making pots, I haven't made that many that I've really liked."

I turn away from the pots and thank him for showing me what he does. In that exact, dry tone, full of meaning but understated, that is present in the precision of the pots and the thoughtfulness of the technique, he says, "You're welcome." We both recognize that this simplicity is exactly enough.

# Marcia Guthrie

**M**arcia Guthrie says she learned the skills of her craft in third grade, or maybe second, but she didn't begin to employ them until about twelve years ago, after she had moved to the Catskills from New York City. One technique is a neat German snowflake fold: A piece of square paper, preferably thin and rather stiff, is folded in half to make a neat rectangle, and the center point of the folded edge is marked. The second fold is made along an imaginary line between the mark and a spot along the other long edge about one quarter of the way from the corner. The third fold mirrors the second, so that the second flap completely covers the first one. These folds should be as crisp as possible. The resulting shape looks something like a stylized tulip, and if the craftsperson begins cutting it, and cuts through every layer, the cut design will be repeated six times. Marcia, however, makes a fourth fold, bisecting the shape from the mark to the V formed by the petals. Now all cuts will be repeated twelve times.

Marcia is a small, dark-haired woman, slender and welcoming. She is modest about her second skill, which is the ability to draw simple figures, and then to transfer them onto the folded paper. "That's the best cow I can make," she says, pointing to a small figure with half moon ears peeping out of a barn door. "And that's absolutely the best chicken. I am not a draw-er. If I were to draw the figures right down on the folded paper, the head could be twice the size of the body, so I draw and erase them until I have a good one, then I transfer that one onto tracing paper and move it around. When I've got it in the right position, I take the pencil and trace it down. All the figures have to touch, too, so that's a reason I have to move them around."

The result, after 4 to 160 hours of design and execution, is an astonishingly complex sort of paper doll—a cut paper picture with intricacy of fine lace, a detailed scene where most of the paper is cut away, leaving a filigree of lines and figures. From the beginning, Marcia was interested in depicting entire worlds. One of her first pictures was of a whole farm: Haystacks run along the bottom, and just above them, a tractor pulls a wagon. Chickens run around between the picket fence and the bottom edge of the barn. The barn door is open, a cow is about to step into the barnyard. The barn siding and the angles of the roof are represented by double narrow cuts. Above the barn, confined by a picket fence, are horses, then trees, and then far fields with sheep in them. The very topmost tier is attached to the picture only by the top of a scarecrow's hat—it is the contour of the distant hills and a row of trees.

Another "world" has a completely different feeling. Marcia calls it *The Heavens*. It is a smaller picture, but also made from a simple six-panel, paper-doll fold: Stars and spherical planets revolve in different directions, their orbits created by thin oval lines. In the lower third of the picture, six stars shoot toward one another, leaving fiery trails. The picture is spikey and energetic, without any of the cosiness of the farm picture, or the whimsicality of the circus (nine rings, clowns, elephants, horses, balloons, parasols, high-wire artists).

Marcia's tools are simple, inexpensive, and unspecialized. An old piece of mat board offers the proper resistance to the X-acto knife (blades, $.30 each). She has been using the same knife handle so long she can't remember where she got it. Paper is a little harder to find, but a 60-foot roll of black (bought through the mail) will last a long time. She prefers the paper to be thin, but six or twelve layers of paper is, after all, only paper. Tracing paper and pencils are readily available almost anywhere. Her studio is an old table in the mud room off the

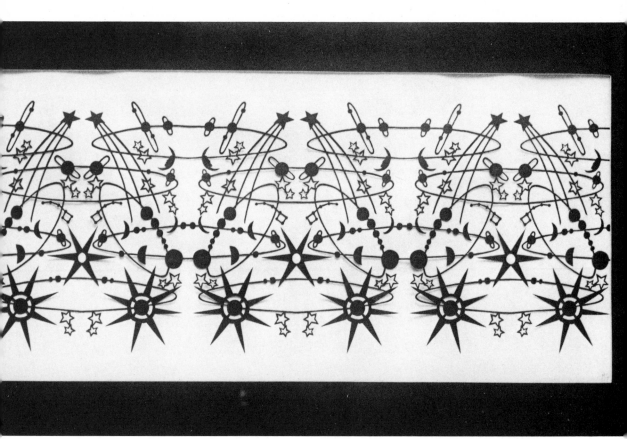

© Jonathan Postma

kitchen. Sometimes she works at the dining-room table. Often there is plenty going on—her eight-year-old daughter, Rosy, is watching TV, or lunch has to be made. David Hayden, Marcia's husband of sixteen years, is in and out. The mother cat leaves her kittens and yowls to go out. Marcia is undistracted—her pictures grow from the pleasures of domestic life, and the fact is that in years and years of making tiny cuts around complex designs, she has never made a mistake, never cut through a slender filament that had been intended to remain.

Marcia discovered and developed her own techniques—for example, she sinks the tips of her X-acto knife into the ending point of the cut she desires to make, then she goes back to the beginning and makes the cut. The cut is finished when the knife falls into the hole. Then she goes back over the same cut as many times as it takes to cut clearly through all twelve or six layers. A row of fence pickets can be cut fairly simply in this way: She makes the six or eight holes, then the six or eight parallel cuts to one side of the pickets, then the holes and the cuts for the other side of the pickets. She cuts across the tops of the pickets, then, more slowly, between the pickets. The paper comes away in a single, toothed section. It is not unlike cutting a jack-o-lantern.

Everything in Marcia's pictures is communicated by shape. She neither draws nor paints anything on the paper, so the figures are like silhouettes. She has turned this limitation greatly to her advantage by using a lot of very small cuts to indicate contours, as well as smiles, eyes, joints, hat brims, and shining surfaces. One of her largest pictures, entitled *The Garden*, is cut from a piece of white paper. A picket fence runs along the bottom. Cats sit on it. In the first row of the garden, carrots and beets grow together, roots and tops neatly differentiated by an impossibly thin strip of white earth. All the vegetables march upward: peppers, more beets, onions with wavy tops, cabbages with five sets of curly leaves made of interior cuts, tomatoes on trellises, a stand of corn tasseled out, two trees, two half trees, and finally, at the top, three suns shedding bright rays over the garden. The rays thicken as

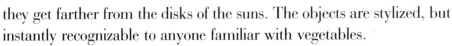

they get farther from the disks of the suns. The objects are stylized, but instantly recognizable to anyone familiar with vegetables.

The key to her precision is the X-acto knife, an instrument that works on the principle of the razor blade. It makes a thin, clear cut, and is easily controlled. Scissors, which most people associate with paper dolls, have a tendency to pinch and bend the paper. Marcia cut her first scene with a pair of scissors, though, and as raggedy as it was, she says, "It didn't have any fine details, but when I opened it out, I loved what it did. It kind of made me go 'Ah!'" She couldn't wait to try again.

Now she sets her folded paper (a small piece of tape holds the fold together) on the mat board. The heel of her hand rests on the table, or carefully on the picture itself. She holds the knife rather as she might hold a pencil, but her forefinger presses down on the upper edge of the knife. The direction of her effort is going to be downward rather than forward. She is left-handed ("a sign of genius," she says, laughing). Sometimes, with her right hand, she steadies the paper. For an especially deep cut, she sometimes uses the strength of her right hand to supplement her left. It is important to make the interior cuts—the eyes and mouth of a cat, for example—before she makes the larger cuts, because when the figures cease being securely attached, cuts are more difficult and the possibility of tearing the figure away from the rest of the picture increases.

She doesn't always make it through every layer on the first cut, and doesn't expect to; after every cut she turns the paper over and checks the bottom to see if the blade has gone all the way through. The result is great uniformity throughout the picture. The only way to tell which layer was originally the top one is to look on the back for the transferred design. People always ask her how she does it. The answer, though Marcia herself is too modest to say so, is that she possesses astonishing patience, and takes a great deal of care with every cut. She says, "Lots of people say to me, 'How come you don't open it up? Can you stand to wait?' And yes, you have to stand to wait, because you can't open it up and then fold it up. You can't open it up until it's all finished." Even a simple design can take ten hours of cutting, spread over a number of days, depending on the number of distractions. Marcia's patience stretches even to cover this mystery—she doesn't know how it will look until every bit of the work is done. But the revelatory moment delights her, just as it did the first time. The only thing she says concerning her own patience is "People say, 'I would go crazy doing this,' but I love it. I just drift. Sometimes I listen to talk radio."

Marcia was born in Westchester, and after college she moved to New York City. She lived there for six years, working mostly for publishing companies. David taught freshman English at Baruch College. Already they had jeopardized their status as future Yuppies by agreeing that each would take two years off to do as he or she pleased, then go back to work while the other one took off. Wasn't she afraid to put her career on hold like that? Marica laughs. "Oh, no! I loved it! I never wanted to go back to an office. And I never did." Instead, she sewed an 18-foot-diameter teepee, and in May of 1973, they took the teepee up to Woodland Valley and pitched it on the banks of the Esopus for four months. "But we could never go back. We abandoned our apartment and he abandoned his job. When it got cold, we knew we would have to find an indoor place, and something to do, and that was the start.

"The teepee was glorious. Someone who came and looked in the door gasped and said, 'This place looks like a maharaja's boudoir!' We bought old Oriental rugs for a buck a foot or something like that. We had all that down, and fur throws. We had a mirror hanging in a tree and David had his typewriter. We had a record player that ran on batteries. We had all the comforts of home." Running water? "We drank the Esopus. This was thirteen years ago, and we were never sick for a day. We learned that you take the water out to bathe, because you don't want to get soap in the water. And certainly we could never go back to West Sixty-fifth Street after that."

Refrigerator? "We dug a hole in the river and we lined it with tall rocks and we put a heavy thing in there, like a gallon of milk. And we had a cooler that we put ice in. And we were only a mile from town, so we could go there every day." She is grinning. "We loved it. Never missed Manhattan for a second. We were finished with that."

When it got cold, they moved to Shandaken, and David went from teaching college to digging rocks: "Because you have to go from city to country. I think he made $2.50 an hour, so we didn't have much cash." They moved in with another couple who had an infant and

© Jonathan Postma

shared expenses. After Shandaken, they lived for five years in Halcott Center. Marcia does not regret the move to the mountains. "It made me strong. I once held up a five-hundred-pound air conditioner, and I loved it that it made me strong. And in so many ways life was much easier in the country. It was as if the mountains were taking away layers of tension, like peeling an onion. I remember walking down the street in Phoenicia, and I was counting my change and putting my money back into my wallet as I was walking down the street. It struck me that I would *never* do that in Manhattan. Right at the counter you get your

money back and count it and put it in your wallet and zip it up, and *then* you walk out in the street. That was when I knew I had changed."

After digging rocks, David worked for nine years sanding and re-finishing floors. Marcia says that the sanding machines were older than he was. His vehicle was a '62 Chevy. Marcia was at home, raising Rosy and, from time to time, trying out ideas and techniques for making cut-out pictures. David's sanding business led to the first recognition of Marcia's work. She says: "I can cut, but I can't push things out of the house. One day, Nancy Harding, from the Roxbury Arts group, came over here, because she wanted the floors done at the Kirkside Retire-ment Home in Roxbury. She said, 'How can I see what your husband does?' and I said, 'Come on over, because he just finished our kitchen floor.' Well, when she got into the mud room, where I was doing my cutting, she said, 'What's this?' and I said, 'Well, I do this.' She said, 'You've got to have a booth at the arts fair.' This must have been eighty-one or so. I was an English major in school. I worked in the editorial department of publishing companies. I'd never had any train-ing, and I thought, well you know, she must know what she's talking about, so I had a booth. And it was wonderful. I sold stuff, people told me my pictures were great. And the next year we had to send slides of our work to be accepted, and I got in again. And not only that, I won a blue ribbon, and I thought, not only was I real, but they thought I was the best. It was one of the most wonderful weekends of my life."

David sold the sanding business about three years ago, "when he could no longer stand it." Now he does some of everything. Marcia works weekends at nearby Kass Inn. They bought a house, but came no closer to the Yuppie ideal: The house, a duplex, cost $6,500. "You can imagine what shape it was in for sixty-five hundred dollars. The bank wasn't going to help us buy it, it looked so terrible." They have removed walls, redone floors, put in a bathroom, remodeled the kitchen. Marcia's studio remains the mud room, though David works in a small outbuilding about fifty yards from the back door. They have tenants in the other side. Rosy frequently plays in the barn loft. They have not abandoned their roots entirely, though—one wall of the living room is books, and there are more groaning bookshelves upstairs. She looks around the sunny room. "You don't have to have a hundred and sixteen thousand dollars to own a house," she says. They even have HBO now, though until three years ago they didn't have a television.

Not long ago, Marcia was asked to do a series of illustrations for an Isaac Bashevis Singer story, "Snow in Chelm," to be included in a school reader put out by Scribner's. She spent fifty-five hours making the designs, after going to the library and looking at pictures of Jewish villages in central Europe during the traditional period that Singer usually writes about. She made a series of six black-on-white pictures: The men of Chelm (traditionally portrayed as fools) gazing in surprise out upon the snow, wearing tall hats that touch the frames of the windows, as they must, and long-tailed coats. The synagogue is unmistakable, down the street. At the bottom of one page, footprints march off through deep snow, effectively rendered by simple cuts. Smoke curls out of village chimneys, anchoring the buildings to the rest of the picture. In another picture, the rays of the sun pour down through the text of the page, melting the amazing snow. It is another world, like *The Heavens* and *The Farm*. The figures of the men, slightly hunched over, look perplexed, old world, a little foolish. They perfectly capture the essence of the Singer story, and they do so entirely by shape. As with the other single pictures, the effect of the myriad details that Marcia has imagined and then realized is astonishing and fascinating.

The cutting took 160 hours, and she worked for the most part without a break—"David took care of everything. He handed in my meals. I worked sixteen hours a day." It was the interest of the work that drove her—aiming for that moment when she could take off the bit of tape, open up the picture, and enter the world she had spent so long creating.

# Everett White

**E**verett White is a short, bearded, slightly built man, round-shouldered, with a quiet manner. He wears a blue T-shirt that reads WOOD-STOCK GLASSWORKS. The back wall of his workshop, which he runs out of the ground floor of the house he rents, is lined with cubbyholes. In each cubbyhole are one or more sheets of glass. He pulls out the most expensive piece he has in the shop, a German "antique" ruby, $10 a square foot. It is a rich, vivid crimson with the telltale imperfections of European glass. Such glass, called antique, though not for its age, is hand-blown in a cylinder about 36 inches long and 18 inches in diameter. When it is still warm and flexible, the cylinder is slit apart and the glass laid out in a sheet. American glass is made in slabs with rollers, rather like pasta. It is more uniform in thickness, but not as vivid.

Even put away in its cubbyholes, the glass looks dangerous to any former child who was sent out of the room if a tumbler broke on the floor. White says, "Don't lean on the table, you'll be picking glass splinters out of your arm." And yet the sheets are lovely, fascinating. Some are swirled with color, like cream in a cup of coffee. "Poorly mixed," says White. Others have a pearly, iridescent surface, painted on the glass and then baked in, a new process. The German and French glass White likes especially has a fascinating depth of color: Held up to the light it *is* light. Round, faceted pieces he has used in the playing cards are called jewels. That's what they look like. Beveled shapes invite the eye to look through them. Custom beveling costs a dollar an inch. For a simple round piece, say 3 inches in diameter, that is about $10.

The very thing that makes each piece of glass intriguing, imperfection, is the thing that makes each piece hard to work with. A piece of glass may vary in tensile strength, brittleness, and thickness, not only from one end to the other, but also from one inch to the next inch. Glass with a streaky color will take different pressures to cut it properly, since the color comes from chemical additives to the glass that change other properties as well. It is only recently that White considers himself to have mastered cutting. He does not think he has necessarily mastered the soldering, although to the untutored eye it looks uniformly well done.

The raw materials of Everett White's craft aren't very raw, not, at least, compared to clay or lumber. As manufactured items, they cost a fair amount, but even so, materials comprise only about 15 percent of the final cost of the piece. Stained glass is labor intensive, and so attaining any kind of profit margin is the result primarily of increasing skill. As the cutter becomes better, he wastes less glass and cuts the pieces so that they will fit more closely together, thus saving money on solder, which is the most expensive raw material. As he becomes better, he works faster. Everett White's business does not support him. When he first moved to Woodstock, it was at a time when land sales were down, and he had been laid off his job as a surveyor on the other side of the Hudson. He sold his house in Pawling, where he was born and grew up, and set up shop. He did fairly well, but, he says, "I couldn't stand the suspense." He is not joking, only reflecting with irony on the general insecurity of the craftsperson's life. Now the business, run only on the weekends, does somewhat more than support itself. It pays for the difference in the rent between having the shop and not, and it supports the raw materials he buys for experimenting with new ideas and new techniques. It keeps him inside on nice days—the possibility of customers means the door is open and he is inside waiting for them. Since he is inside he is at work, and the more work he does the more the business pays for itself. So this year, once again, he won't quit. Besides, if he quit making stained glass as a business, he would just make it as a hobby. Meanwhile, land sales are up. He could survey the land between the river and the Connecticut border, down to Putnam County, and north to about Hudson seven days a week, if he wanted to. But he doesn't.

On the work table, laid together in preparation for soldering, are two windows. One is the figure of the King of Spades, and one is the figure of the Queen of Hearts. There are over a hundred pieces in each window. Everett gets his designs from a variety of sources, but he especially loves Victorian glass, and Victorian design is his main inspiration. These windows, a commission, began as a small sketch, which Everett finds easier to work with. Once he has drawn his design, he uses an opaque projector to enlarge it to the size he desires—he projects it onto a large sheet of brown paper, and draws over the lines. This drawing he copies, using carbon paper, onto another piece of brown paper. The last copy is called the *cartoon.*

It used to be that Everett cut out his cartoon with a pair of razor blades taped together and held slightly apart by a spacer, but about five years ago, pattern shears, a specialized tool for stained-glass makers,

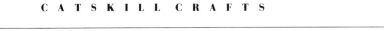

came onto the market. Pattern shears have three parallel blades, and when he is finished cutting apart the pattern pieces, there will be $\frac{1}{32}$ inch between all of them, room for the solder. The purpose of this kind of precision is to keep the window from growing larger as he puts the pieces together, and to keep all the pieces in the proper proportion to one another.

The glass cutting is the part of the operation that Everett finds challenging and enjoys the most. His tool is called, simply, a glass cutter, and it looks like a small pizza wheel. The edge of the cutting wheel is either stainless steel or carbide. Each glass cutter costs about $7, and lasts about a week, if he works all week. The cutting life of a wheel is partly determined by the hardness of the glass Everett is cutting. Reds and oranges are especially hard, ambers and browns rather soft. The cutting takes some strength, and a constant sense of appropriate pressure. At the end of a day of cutting, he says, "The tip of my finger is numb, and stays that way for a few hours."

Choosing pleasing colors and cutting and breaking the glass are simultaneous operations—he will change his mind about colors that he has expected to use as he goes through the cubbyholes and sees others that please him. Once he chooses a piece, he lays the pattern piece on it, holds it down with one hand, and runs the cutter around it with the other. The cutter scores the glass, making a row of tiny little breaks in the surface, and it is along this weakness that Everett will break the glass. He breaks it as soon as he scores it. If he were to leave it alone, even for five minutes, it would begin to heal itself. If he set it aside for an hour, it would be as difficult to break as if he had never scored it in the first place. It is not the shape that Everett makes that dictates how easily the glass will break along the proper line, but the imperfections of the glass. "Glass always takes the path of least resistance," he says, and this path is slightly unpredictable. Nevertheless, most straight lines and gentle curves are fairly straightforward. A circle or a tight inside curve demands its own techniques. For a circle, Everett uses a circle cutter, which is a glass cutter that looks and works like a compass. This is used to make the first score. After that, he makes three or four straight cuts radiating outward from the circle. These are called the break-out lines. He resents the break-out lines a little. "I always have to see if I can do it in one piece," he says.

Another new tool introduced since Everett began making stained glass is a water-cooled diamond grinder. This is a small, motor-driven wheel, about an inch in diameter, that sits in a little trough of water and protrudes above a little table. It spins at about 1,500 RPM, and uses a diamond abrasive to smooth the edges of the cut glass, or the little pieces that always remain when the cutter has cut a piece that comes to a sharp angle. Everett used to trim unevenness spots, or "nibble away at them" with a sort of pliers. Ironically, if the jagged spot projected, say, a quarter of an inch, Everett could trim it fairly easily, but if it projected only a thirty-second of an inch, he could not, and would have to cut another piece. It is this sort of waste that Everett saves himself with the grinder now, but he is proud of the precision of his cutting, and mentions that some glassmakers use the grinder more to shape the pieces than simply to smooth them down, making up for their lack of expertise in cutting.

As he cuts the pieces, he lays them out on his sketch, to make sure that they fit together.

The copper foil method of stained glass making was invented by Tiffany in the late nineteenth century, and is the most commonly used method today, because it has a number of advantages over the Medieval method, where each piece of glass was puttied into lead *cames*. The first of these is strength. A Tiffany window can support itself and, properly installed, will probably never need repairs. Second, and more important from an artistic point of view, it gives the glassmaker greater control over the small, acutely angled pieces of the design. When bent too sharply, lead cames tend to kink; with the Tiffany method, any piece that the glassmaker can get foil around, he can include in the design.

Pre-Tiffany glass has a lot of the detail painted on, because small pieces of glass are so difficult to lead. Post-Tiffany glassmakers need not bother with painting if they don't want to, although Everett is beginning to experiment with certain effects: The faces and hands of his King and Queen are painted.

With all the advantages of the copper foil method of putting glass together, it still used to be the step that Everett hated the most about making stained glass. He says, "I used to get all of the kids in the neighborhood to do it." The copper foil came in sheets, like aluminum foil, and first had to be carefully cut into strips. Then he would hold each piece up to the light and fit the strips of foil around it, making sure that just enough foil covered both edges. It was time-consuming and tedious and left his fingertips full of little cuts. Now foil comes in rolls of strips, already provided with adhesive. These are fitted to the foiling machine, which neatly wraps the edges of each piece just so. Everett estimates that the foiling machine, which he got some 5 or 6 years ago, saves him 60 to 70 percent of the time he used to spend. As he foils, he replaces the pieces on the pattern, and when he is done foiling, he is ready to solder.

The pieces of the two playing cards don't fit together exactly. It is in the spaces between the pieces that the solder will flow when Everett solders them together, first on one side and then on the other. All traces of the copper will be covered, and the lines of solder will be smooth and even, about a sixteenth of an inch in width. The solder is a 50/50 mix of lead and tin, though sometimes Everett uses different mixes, depending how quickly he want to solder to harden. Everett always solders the entire piece at once, partly to get it over with, and partly because the soldering doesn't require much thinking. He can contemplate other things, as long as he keeps a steady hand. The melted solder runs out of the gun quickly, not like honey, but like water. He uses a 150- to 250-Watt soldering iron, with a rheostat, to maintain the solder at a constant temperature. Unsteadiness or slowness shows on the piece—the soldering appears to have a rippled effect, and this can't be corrected, because the solder cools and hardens within seconds. In fact, some of the other mixes he uses cool instantly. When he is finished with one side, he slides it to the end of the table, and, using the table edge as a support, he upends the piece and turns it over. He is careful, but not overly worried—with only one side soldered, the window is nearly as strong as it will be when he is finished. Only with especially big windows does he take more precautions: These he slips onto a piece of plywood, and then, as if they were large potato pancakes, he flips them gently over. For all practical purposes, the window is finished, except that Everett dislikes the bright silver of the solder and prefers to wash it with an antiquing solution that will blacken it. He does not install the windows. Once they are out the door they are out of his hands. He would rather leave the installation to an experienced carpenter. The windows are not delicate. They need be handled only with the same amount of care as any regular sheet of glass. Just one has come back to him, and that was because someone sat on it.

Everett has been making stained glass for twelve or thirteen years. When he started, there were few books on the subject—stained glass had gone out of fashion with, literally, a crash—the sound of big, beautiful Tiffany windows being broken up and thrown out all through the forties and fifties. There were glassmakers who knew how to do it but, as Everett says, "They weren't telling." What Everett wanted was a stained glass hanging lamp, then quite a fashion, but he couldn't afford the price. He worked out the method for making one himself, a large round lampshade with a rose motif along the border. Now he says, "It would have been cheaper to buy that one." Now he doesn't make himself anything. He says, "I can't afford stained glass."

Although Everett balks at calling himself an artist—he doesn't think he is as creative as an artist would be—it is actually the designing of the window, and to a lesser extent, the cutting of the glass, that interests him. By the time the window is laid out on the table, he is already

turning new projects over in his mind. Seventy-five percent of his business is on commission, and it is those projects that he is thinking about. Now he glances around and dismisses everything on display in his shop. It is all routine, here to give passersby something to look at or buy, if they want it, perhaps to show that this is a professional establishment rather than a hobby. Sometimes a customer comes in and orders a piece of glass, just because he or she has seen a box or a mirror Everett sold a year or two ago. Where the other commissions come from he isn't exactly sure. If he were, all his business would be commissions.

There are plenty of new techniques that Everett would like to get around to teaching himself. He has begun to do etched glass, which is called sandblasting. He paints adhesive vinyl over a design he has made in the glass, then uses an X-acto knife to cut out the design. Now he can either strip off the vinyl covering the design or the vinyl around the design, depending whether he wants a positive or negative effect. After that, he sends the piece of glass to a friend of his who makes tombstones, and the friend sandblasts it in his sandblasting room. Recently, Everett has tried a technique of directly fusing glass to glass. Usually the differing chemical properties of various pieces of glass mean that they melt and harden at slightly different temperatures, and so glass can't be fused to glass either edge to edge or surface to surface. This new technique, which uses a special kind of glass whose melting characteristics have been made uniform across the color spectrum, opens up a huge number of possibilities, but so far he hasn't had the time to make any real pieces, only to try out the properties of the glass.

It is not that he doesn't like surveying. The survey crew works year around these days, rain and snow. He says, "I complain sometimes if it's been raining a lot, but after they've put me on the computer or had me drawing plans for three days, I want to get back out again. Even chopping down underbrush. I feel like an explorer." He knows the landscape of Dutchess County pretty well by now and likes it a lot. He knows the west side of the river less well, though he likes to hike and camp. Is he in the Catskills or the Hudson Valley? The land surveyor speaks: "I suppose if you're on a boat in the middle of the river, you're in the Hudson Valley. But on land, you're in the Catskills."

Woodstock has changed since the land boom. The building to Everett's left, the old railroad station, is vacant and for sale. The owner wants a quarter of a million dollars. Another house, to the right, can be had for $350,000. Prices have only really jumped like this in the last couple of years, but it's obvious that a craftsman can't support himself by making Tiffany lamps or leather checkbook covers with those sort of mortgage payments. Everett rents, and he can afford his rent still, but it may be that he will soon be driven out of Woodstock, as other crafts-people have been. He says, "What will they have then? This is why people want to come to Woodstock, because of the artists and craftsmen. Already some of the stores are branches of other stores elsewhere." I look around, down the street. It's true. Woodstock reminds me not a little of Southampton.

But for now, Everett White can still bear the suspense. He has one dealer in New York for whom he makes a lot of boxes and Christmas things every year, and he has enough commissions. After the King and Queen, he will begin a sandblasting project, two door lights, 13 inches wide by 58 inches long, with a complicated Victorian design. The design will be clear, the background opaque. While the designing of the windows and the transfer of the design will take him three days of work, the sandblasting will only take half an hour. Other projects await, too. The little shop is a pleasing and colorful spot, hung with bright mirrors and lampshades, paneled in dark wood. The glass in the cubbyholes and lying on the table gives it the air of a Medieval workshop, and there is a kind of purity to the setting, to Everett's devotion to his craft. If such people were driven out of Woodstock by a department store, it would be a shame indeed.

# Lesly Charles

**O**nce Lesly Charles was in the business of making "seconds." He and a partner would make a handful of perfect pots for display and make lots of allegedly less perfect ones, which they stacked together and labeled seconds. These they priced somewhat lower than the displayed price of the "perfect" pots. Probably all of the wares were much the same—Lesly is skilled at making pots—but the customers were so pleased at the prospect of getting a bargain that they couldn't get enough of the seconds. Lesly got out of the seconds business because he couldn't keep up with demand. After that, he got out of New York City, and moved to Phoenicia, where he has his studio, Maidstone Ceramics, in the living room and kitchen of his house.

His methods are still geared to production in a way that the methods of craftspersons with another source of income are not, and the fact is that he takes an engineer's interest in production itself—not only of pottery, but of bricks, of statuary, of anything that might lend itself to being made more quickly, without appreciable loss of quality. In his studio, a dark, dusty room that looks out a bay window upon Route 214, the potter's wheel is pushed out of the way. The electric kiln almost blocks the doorway to the former kitchen, and the most important piece of equipment is unobtrusively screwed to the frame of the doorway to the front hall. It is an extruder, a square tube about 4 × 4 inches, and some 18 inches long. In the bottom, there is a plate with sixteen ridged holes in it, each about 1½ inches long and ½ inch wide. At the top, a lever, some 2½ feet long, is attached to the plunger. As Lesly says, "It is a very, very crude machine." It works on the cookie press principle, and from the ridged strips that are extruded, Lesly weaves basketlike pots of all shapes and sizes, from shallow, rectangular gratin dishes to tall, round flowerpots.

His material is red stoneware, and he buys it de-aired. It is a grainy, coarse clay. He rips away the cardboard box and the moisture-proof plastic and stands the block of clay up on the big work table. With a long-bladed knife, he quickly slices the clay into four pieces that approximate the size of the extruder. Each will become one pot. Now he raises the handle of the extruder, loads the clay, and pulls the handle down with a single, quick motion. The ridged strips squeeze out of the bottom, and swing slightly with the energy of Lesly's motion. He gathers them together and moves them over to the table with the delicacy and care of a person gathering damp pasta—he doesn't want them to stick together, break, or lose the definition of the ridges. It is these ridges that give the finished pots the illusion of being made of rushes, an illusion so strong that more than one person, upon first seeing them, must reach out and touch them to make sure they are pottery.

He uses plaster molds to define the precise shape of each pot, and he has sets of these under the table. He decides to make a dish and chooses a round, shallow mold. He has been making pots in this woven style for five years now, and he begins with practised expertise, laying the first strip across the diameter of the pot, pushing off each end of the strip with his thumb, like someone making pie crust. He lays another strip across this one at an angle of about 30 degrees, then a third next to and parallel to the first. The third strip covers the second, which covers the first. With deft, quick pressings of his thumb, he pushes the strips together, causing the clay to adhere, but never appreciably denting the

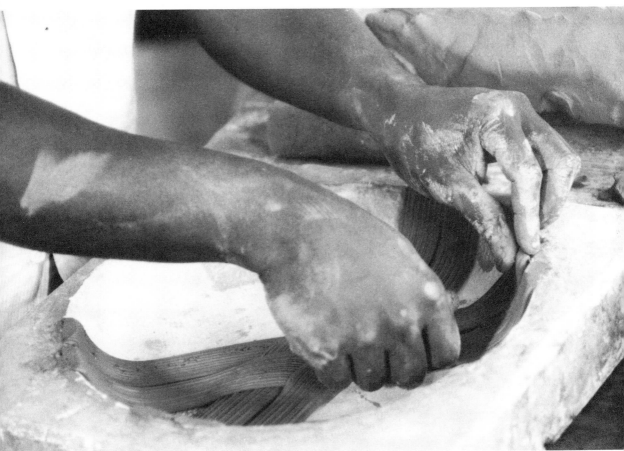

© Michael Owen

© Michael Owen

pattern of ridges. The fourth strip goes down beside the second, over the third. Now he carefully folds the first strip back and positions the fourth strip beneath it. After it is laid, each strip is pinched off at the edge of the mold, and so the weaving grows neatly. The strips become progressively smaller, the weaving progressively more complex, but the pot doesn't take long, maybe 15 minutes. Lesly chats easily—his hands seem to do all the work and to note all the peculiarities of the clay. He makes the most use possible of the limited elasticity of the clay, turning pieces back and laying them down again, and there is nothing that he has to do twice or repair. Each strip lies flat next to its neighbor. The weaving is tight—although the clay will shrink in firing, the pot will hold food when it is finished. Finally, he takes a knife and gives the edge a last smoothing. A bit of clay drops onto the inside of the dish. He doesn't touch it. When the clay has dried, in a day or so, to leatherlike hardness, he will be able to pick this bit off the bowl. If he were to do so now, he might dent the ridges and ruin his design.

He takes down another mold, this one oval, and pushes another fourth of the original block of clay through the extruder. The molds are precisely sized. Not much of the clay is wasted or left to be used again.

A feature of Lesly's pots that is especially striking is the voluptuous use of leaves and other vegetable forms to set off the precision of the weaving. They seem to grow out of the rims of the pots and to cling to their sides as if growing there. Sometimes, these plants form the handles as well as the decoration. Lesly's favorite forms, lately, are large cucumber leaves, acorns, asparagus, and small ears of corn. He also uses plaster molds for these forms. He begins by gathering leaves or acorns or other shapes that both interest him and have distinct contours that can be picked up by the plaster. He is especially fond of the cucumber leaves because of their large size and their prominent veins. He gathers a few good specimens, lays them out, paints on some plaster, and waits for it to dry. Voilà, a mold.

When a pot has dried sufficiently to accept decoration, Lesly rolls a bit of leftover clay into one of the molds, scrapes away the excess, then eases the clay out of the mold. With a few deft motions, he gives the leaf contour, ever careful of the design formed by the leaf veins, which he would like to preserve. He applies the leaf to the side of the pot with slip, a liquid mixture of clay and water, and tests it with his fingers to make sure it is firmly attached. Then he rolls another bit of clay onto a old piece of shingle. This will be the long strip of the vine that twines from the base of each leaf around the circumference of the pot. His motion as he applies these decorations is quick, firm patting. He is always aware of what this particular piece of clay needs to make it adhere or to give it an interesting shape. He says, "It's got to have a certain kind of movement to give you the feeling of dark and light, and of drama." There are some forms he has tried that don't work, such as mushrooms, but he is always on the lookout for new possibilities.

Lesly makes a variety of pots, not all of them woven. He casts dishes of the same shape as the woven ones in his molds, and then glazes the inside surfaces, and he also throws large amphoralike vases on the wheel. These stand about 16 inches high right now, although he would like to be making 4-foot ones. Sometimes he glazes these, and sometimes he half-glazes them in shiny black, blue, gray, green, or yellow. The recurring motif is the leaf and vine—the vases look almost stark without it. He paints the glazes on, and the colors are bright and flat, unsubtle but striking. More delicate but no less arresting are his asparagus bowls. At first glance, the rim seems unadorned, but then the curving asparagus present themselves, slender, neat, appetizing. The bowl asks to have soup poured into it. Lately, he has been trying out ears of corn partially hidden in corn leaves. The effect is dynamic and sensual. Lesly casts a lot of shapes—celery leaves, pea pods, maple and oak leaves, fish—just to see how they come out and whether they can be made to work with the pots. The most satisfactory so far is the

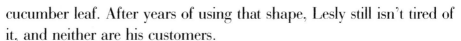

cucumber leaf. After years of using that shape, Lesly still isn't tired of it, and neither are his customers.

Haitian by birth, Lesly came with his family to New York City in 1969, when he was nine years old. His mother was Irish, a textile artist who had died in Haiti a year or so before from the combined effects of pneumonia and bad medical care. Lesly says his father, a banker, was forced out of Haiti. Lesly grew up in New York City and went to the Fashion Institute of Technology, to study textile design. He did some free lancing for a while, but says, "It seemed that I was not a very commercial painter or textile designer, but I apprenticed under several good sculptors in New York City and discovered that I see things better in a three-dimensional way than in a two-dimensional way." Even now, his special fondness is for metal casting, and pottery is, to some extent, a substitute for bronze and metal sculpture.

In the late seventies, he went to work as a designer for Terra Firma Ceramics, on Twenty-fifth Street. At Terra Firma, they were trying out techniques for weaving pots, and Lesly, with his textile experience, was able to refine and develop their ideas. Later, the owners of Terra Firma wanted to drop the woven line, but Lesly didn't consider that he had learned as much from it, or done as much with it, as he could. He parted from them and moved to Phoenicia three years ago. When he talks about lessons he has learned that are important to him, they almost always have to do with learning how to market his work, or with learning how to produce it faster, possibly the influence of his years at F.I.T. That his work has been sold at Bergdorf's, Tiffany's, and other prestigious outlets seems unimportant to him—his work has always sold well and impressed people, and he understands that Bergdorf's was not selling his work to do him a favor.

Some years ago, Lesly and a friend from Santo Domingo, Arturo Cruez, made a series of tea cups with running greyhounds as the handles. He says, "We decided we would hang out in the Village and produce potteries. We were so stupid as kids, our goal was to only produce fifty dollars a week to eat and that was it. We had a buyer, and the price on the cups was eight dollars. The guy loved it, but he only wanted to give us three dollars for them. Arturo decided to teach the guy a lesson, so he set up a blanket out in front of the guy's shop, on Sixth Avenue, and put all the cups out. In a half an hour, most of the cups were sold, and there were only eight left. Then the guy decided to take the eight that were left for his own personal use. The lesson that taught me was that you don't have to give in to people, your work is fine enough by itself."

He has learned other lessons. For example, he is very enthusiastic about his extruder, and the industrial purposes it could be put to, with a little imagination. Brick making, for example. Right now, bricks are made in molds, one at a time. How much less expensive would it be if they were just plopped out of extruders onto moving belts? And speaking of bricks, why stop at rectangular bricks that depend on mortar to hold them together? Why not have interlocking bricks, maybe made of plastic, that would hold themselves together, but also have some flexibility? Where would they be useful? Perhaps in earthquake-prone tropical countries, where earth is plentiful and other building materials scarce? It is an idea he works on sometimes. A roll of technical drawings sits on a shelf near the extruder. Or spray metallizing. What could be done with that, besides patching elderly bronze statues? Can his designs, which work so well in clay, be produced in pewter, or in glass? Why not?

He also teaches. He spent a number of years teaching pottery in special education classes, and he is good at it—encouraging and patient. He does not hesitate before allowing the seven-year-old to work at the wheel—certainly the most fascinating and magical piece of potter's equipment, for which hand building can be no substitute in the seven-year-old mind. They sit across from one another, the wheel about knee

level between them. He leans toward the student and speaks in an even, patient voice, asking her if she has ever thrown a pot before. She has not. He starts the wheel and throws a blob of clay into the center. As he centers it and cones it up, he explains what they are going to do, in a voice low enough to attract and hold her attention. He demonstrates— his palms and fingers hold the clay, his thumbs shape it. She watches. Does she understand? She nods, predictably. He says, "Can you center it?" She hesitates, wishing to, but afraid, and as firmly and unaggressively as possible, he takes her hands and positions them on the clay, holding them and showing her how to shape the mound, then how to pull out the sides. When her hands get dry, he dips them in the water bowl. They make four small pots, and he has her attention the whole time, always talking about what they are doing, about being gentle with the clay, and not doing anything sudden. He lets her try shaping the pot herself, but when it looks like it might break, he helps her again, showing where to put her hands, not letting her fail or get nervous. At the end of four pots, she feels accomplished and happy. The lesson is successful because he has made her sense how it is done. He has also let her make as many pots as she wants to, without making her feel that she must hurry or stop before she gets her fill.

Lesly does not have the problem that some craftspersons have, of finding a receptive audience for his work. Everything he makes is shipped out within days after the kiln is opened. That suits him. He says, when asked what his favorite part of the process is, "When I sell it or give it away. I don't feel that I'm producing it for myself. I don't like to touch the clay, but I touch it. It's just a magnet that brings us together." If a design he comes up with isn't popular, he feels no qualms about dropping it, but at the same time, he considers himself an artist: "After you make the first hundred thousand, some people may see it as a craft, but when I do something, I try to keep the same artistic feeling from the first to the millionth." Now he would rather like to have a

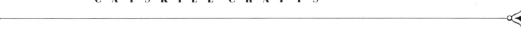

store of his own, partly to have more control over the business side of his craft, but also to have closer contact with those who use his pots: "I'm sort of bored with the market. These works have been everywhere over the years, and the only thing left is to have my own stores, in order to be able to get the sort of feedback that I wanted to know about the work rather than a second-hand feedback. Even if they don't like it, I want to know why they don't like it. I want to make it work for them."

He would like the customer to get close to the work. He says, "The work really wants to be touched. I have to bring it to a level where people have to touch it, and use it, and even break it. Part of the reason I left New York was that people were buying the work but not using it." He would like to refine the baskets—make them lighter, less apparently pottery: "You should be able to see it as natural baskets, and it's not until you really come up to it and feel that it is ceramics that you know. The weight should be considerably less."

Although he shares nothing with Michael Boyer in terms of technique, working style, or professional goals, Lesly does have some of the same reflective habits. Maybe it is part of being a potter. He says, "When you are making a pot on the wheel, and have your hands on the clay, you have to be careful of what you think, because everything you think is instantly reflected in the work. There should be a lie-detector test where the person has to have his hands on clay on a wheel. He would be instantly revealed." He smiles. He thinks a lot about production, about technique, about shipping orders, about selling his designs to larger companies and having them produced in other materials, about whether he is getting a fair monetary return for his efforts. He does what many craftsmen hate to do, which is to make the same pot over and over. Someday, he might actually weave his hundred thousandth dish, by hand, but, he says, "I see myself as an artist, and even when I'm producing what seems to be craft, I see it as art, because the feeling that I put in each particular piece is just a phenomenal feeling that I get when I put my hand on something and start to manipulate things to make them work for me. I lose all sense and go into a state where I just forget everything. What I really feel is a sense of beauty and of love in the thing that I'm doing, and this is what I'm trying to get across. Everything becomes special—the line no longer is just a line, it becomes a special line—and I see how it relates to everything—to the classic past, to the future."

# Howard Bartholomew

About four years ago, Howard Bartholomew decided to cut down one of the black walnut trees in his backyard. Each year, that particular tree dropped its leaves before the others, and he suspected that it had been struck by lightning some years before and damaged. The tree was one of a cluster of four huge walnuts, each some 3 to 4 feet in diameter, that Howard estimates are about 150 years old. There are nine others on the property, some planted by Howard and some growing from squirrel caches. Howard's trees are in turn part of a grove of black walnuts that, he thinks, predates the founding of Middleburgh. The grove meanders along the banks of Schoharie Creek for about 20 miles, and many of the trees are healthy monsters. Black walnuts are well known to gardeners because their roots exude a toxic substance known as juglone, which is lethal to the nightshade family and to apple trees. Black walnuts make a place for themselves in the forest, and no pests, as yet, seem to harm them.

On Thanksgiving of that year, he cut down the tree and sawed it into 8-foot lengths. The following Monday, he took a day off from his job teaching American history at Schoharie Central School and went with the logs to the lumber mill to watch them be lumbered. Of black walnut, he says, "As good friends as you are with any sawyer, it's like a cat around shrimp, you've got to be there, or some of it is going to disappear." He laughs. He had the planks cut varying thicknesses, from 1¼ inches to 4 inches.

Howard knew exactly what to do with the fallen tree, and now what he did with it stands under the front windows of the living room—a Chippendale lowboy, dark and satiny. The finished lowboy is a subtly spectacular piece. The four dragon claw–and–ball feet and the delicate, deeply curved legs seem almost ready to leap off the floor. The scallop shell carving into the middle drawer repeats the motif of the lower scrollwork. The two front posts are fluted columns set into the corners. The pulls are of bright brass (the only metal in the piece), and the top, so smooth and chocolaty that it begs to be stroked, is finished with an old-fashioned stain made of walnut shells soaked in water and mixed with a little beet juice to give it a reddish tint. The walnut shells he picked out of his driveway—that is where he throws the walnuts every year to be husked as people drive in and out; otherwise, the husks are so hard that it is nearly impossible to take them off. He is rather proud of the lowboy, especially of the legs, which are each carved from a single block of black walnut. He is also proud of the fluted corner columns and the spaces that he painstakingly carved out for them.

The lowboy is not the only piece in the living room that Howard has done. Corner cabinets, one of pine with a scallop shell inset and another of cherry with an arched-top door and a pediment top stand to either side of it. Howard's Windsor writing chair is near the sofa. In the front hall, across from an antique Chippendale writing desk, is the first piece

Stained glass by Everett White, at the Reservoir Inn, West Hurley, Ulster County

Farm scene, taken near Vega Mountain, Town of Roxbury, Delaware County

Bull thistle (*Cirsium vulgare*), taken near Fleischmanns, Town of Middletown, Delaware County

Evening primroses (*Oenothera biennis*), taken near Frost Valley, Ulster County

Teapot, porcelain, Laura Wilensky

*Cookies at Fritz's Place*, porcelain, Henry Cavanagh

A pair of eastern gobblers, wood and metal, 1984, Ward Herrmann

Miniature Oriental chest (scale 1 inch to 12 inches), Rosemarie Torre

A view of the Pepacton Reservoir in the fog, from the Route 30 bridge, between Margaretville and Downsville, Town of Andes, Delaware County

A view of the Ashokan Reservoir, Ulster County

Tree fungus, variety unknown, taken near Frost Valley

Near John Burroughs Memorial field, Town of Roxbury, Delaware County

Along Roses Brook Road, Town of Stamford, Delaware County

of furniture Howard ever made, seven years ago, and that is a Queen Anne chest-on-chest, a highboy, 7 feet high, twelve drawers, all cherry and bird's-eye maple. It is easy to see one thing that the antique and the new piece have in common—sharply defined sliding dovetails that hold everything together. The maker of the antique made no effort to conceal these in the top of his writing desk, and neither has Howard—they are a feature of American Chippendale that not only flaunts the exactness of the joints but also makes decorative use of the contrasting colors of the woods used—in this case, cherry and curly maple.

In the dining room is a piece that Howard especially likes because he made it partly of firewood. It is a bench that is actually four chairs in a row, called a deacon's bench. Each section shares its arms with the sections next to it. The front legs of the bench are set under the arms, but the back legs are set in the middle of each back. It is a more rustic piece, simpler, coarser, painted green. The oddly set back legs almost give it a sense of playfulness.

It is obvious that Howard especially likes the woods that are native to his native soil. Stacked in his workshop are more planks of the walnut tree—"Look at that grain," he says, pulling one out. "That's limb wood. It's the crotch that gives it that lovely pattern." Behind the walnut are pieces of cherry, maple, butternut, pine. He discovers each one with a sense of pleasure in the unique qualities of the wood. The bottoms of the drawers in the chest? "Oh, that's basswood. Lovely wood to work with. Very light." When two men bring a trailer load of firewood for the wood-burning furnace, Howard has them stack it any old way. He intends to split it, for one thing, but also to look through for especially straight-grained pieces that might be of use as chair legs, chair arms, whatever. None of this firewood will go unappreciated. Above his woodpile is a small sign: OLD WOOD TO BURN, OLD WINE TO DRINK, OLD BOOKS TO READ, OLD FRIENDS TO TRUST.

Howard is a purist. He takes his designs from the three-volume catalogue of American furniture from the seventeenth to the early nine-

teenth centuries, put together and published in the 1920s by Wallace
Nutting. "Nutting did the same thing for American furniture that Alan
Lomax did for American folk music," says Howard, and it was a
monumental undertaking—5,000 pages of black-and-white photographs of all sorts of American furniture from the Colonial and Fed-
eralist periods, with dimensions and, in some cases, detailed
measurements of particular parts. Nutting also gathered together a
large furniture collection for J. P. Morgan, the financier. Fortunately for
Nutting, and Morgan, a great many of the early pieces were still around
then, and their designs were preserved. Fortunately for Howard Bartholomew, too, since he considers the Chippendale period the best period of furniture making, and doesn't care to reinvent the wheel by
designing his own. If one of Nutting's photographs includes the overall
dimensions of the piece, Howard can reproduce it. He is always careful
to sign the piece and label it as a reproduction.

Howard likes the furniture he has made and is naturally proud of it,
but what he loves is the tools. His workshop is a small shed, 16 × 18
feet, that stands at the back of the property. East- and south-facing
windows look out upon a neat grove of black walnuts planted by Howard's neighbor. Beyond them rises the profile of a mountain locally
known as The Cliff. Along the north wall is Howard's workbench and,
above it, rows of the hand-held planes and chisels and knives that he
prefers to use. There is a vise at each end of the workbench, one for
Howard, to the left, and one for his eight-year-old son, Alex, to the
right. Various pictures attest to Howard's allegiances: Alex, at two and a
half, planting a pumpkin seed in the garden, an American flag, a
painting of Christ in the Garden of Gethsemane with the legend, "Call
unto me, And I will answer thee, and show the great and mighty
things, which thou knowest not," seven men at a hunting camp, trying
out sites and getting ready to go out, the head of a buck, an old adver-
tisement for shotgun shells.

The carving Howard does is not whittling, and the key to its precision is the variety of planes, gouges, chisels, and other carving tools that he uses, tools that were designed for making the sort of furniture he likes to make, which is notable for decoration as well as grace of design. Planes, as the name indicates, are for shaping flat surfaces. He selects a piece of pine and clamps it in the vise between two smaller pieces of basswood, edge upward. The plane he uses is a Stanley, of a style Stanley ceased manufacturing sometime in the fifties. The key to the molding is in the shape of the cutting edge, which protrudes forward about ⅛ inch from the sole plate. He sets the sole plate at one end of the narrow strip of pine and pushes it forward, excavating a groove about 1/16 inch from the edge of the board. He does it again, and then again, and soon the surface to the right of the groove begins to have a curve to it. The groove itself deepens, becomes **V**-shaped. Each shaving comes off in a blond, tissue-thin curl. Howard's motion is steady, but he is not especially exerting himself. The groove helps guide the cutting edge, the keenness of the cutting edge saves effort. Eight or ten careful but quick passes transform the plank into the beginnings of a molding. If he wants to make it more elaborate, he can take another plane, with a differently shaped cutting edge, and modify what he's done, or add to it. Each pass is so conservative, does so little, that it is more difficult to make a mistake than not to make one, and that is what Howard especially likes about using these old tools, that they enable him to take care.

But Howard's pieces have many curved edges, turned pieces, and rounded, carved ornaments, called finials. It is, perhaps, the variety of these that keeps him interested, and the challenge of discovering (re-discovering) techniques that give a certain effect without excessive, onerous labor on Howard's part. After the walnut lumber had dried, for example (about eighteen months of air drying, stickered—stacked in layers of planks separated by sticks—then four or five months "down cellar" until the moisture content was about 8 percent), before beginning the lowboy, he spent his time figuring out how he was going

to carve the legs and feet, because he was already familiar with the techniques he would use to build the cabinet and the drawers. In fact, each of the legs took him some twenty hours from the time he first traced the shape of the leg on the 3 × 5 × 35-inch block of wood. The overall shape of the leg he made with a draw knife—a tool with two parallel handles and a curved blade that is pulled toward the furniture maker—and a spoke shave—another sort of draw knife that makes narrower strokes. After that, he gouged and chiseled out the finer details of the shape—the acanthus leaf at the top and the ball and claw at the bottom—and, in fact, had one of his gouges remade by a blacksmith so that it could cut in the right sort of curve. The legs turned out to be no easier than he had foreseen—one of them warped when the interior moisture was exposed to the air and another turned out to be wormy. One trick that his grandfather taught him—using a piece of broken glass to smooth the ball into roundness—came in especially handy.

© Michael Owen

To ensure that all of the angles in the chest were exact, Howard either stacked pieces and cut them at the same time, or he cut a single, thick piece and then ripped it into two thinner pieces. This second method is how he cut the apron and the back so that they would match, and also how he cut the dovetails on the sides of the drawers. To attempt to measure as exactly as this would be almost inevitably a losing proposition, and it is for this reason that Howard likes to have the wood custom-sawed into very thick planks, although it costs more per board foot. In addition, thicker planks can be planed if they warp without fear of getting them too thin.

The legs are attached to the sides by hunch mortises, a series of crenulations that offer the glue plenty of surface to cling to. In modern furniture, these crenulations are often absent, somewhat weakening the joint or rendering it extremely dependent upon the adhesive strength of the glue. The fluted quarter columns were another detail, like the legs, that Howard gave a lot of thought to. Finally, he glued together three pieces of wood, with paper in between them. A half round served as the anchor for two quarter rounds, and this entire piece was turned on the lathe, then carved. The cylinder was popped apart, the half round set aside, and the two exactly similar quarter rounds set into the corners Howard had gouged out for them.

The top is made of two planks of walnut, one 16 inches wide and one 10 inches. These were doweled together, that is, shallow holes were drilled in the sides of each, then short pieces of dowel were inserted into each pair of holes, once again giving the glue more surface area to cling to. The top was then planed as a single piece and pinned to the cabinet. The stain of walnut and beet juice was applied, then Howard began the long process of finishing the wood.

Well-finished wood, of course, lasts longer and is more beautiful than unfinished wood. For one thing, wood soaks up moisture in the summer and dries up in the winter, putting stress on furniture joints. A carefully applied finish inhibits the wood from taking in extra moisture.

It also affords a harder surface—shedding blows that might otherwise cause nicks, puddling water droplets that might otherwise soak in. A good finish also highlights the grain and makes something beautiful out of the natural quality of the wood. There are two types of finishes—those that release solvents into the air, getting lighter as they dry, and those that oxidize, changing their chemical composition by taking oxygen from the air and getting heavier as they dry. One of the latter, tung oil, is what Howard used on the lowboy, painting it on, then letting it dry and harden, then rubbing it off with sandstone and pumice mixed with mineral oil and applied with a felt pad. Although the instructions say that the tung oil should be allowed to dry for twenty-four hours, Howard waited, especially in the latter coats, for five to seven days before sanding off each coat. At last he applied a hard vegetable wax called Antiquax, and the piece was finished—about two hundred hours of work, not including the lumbering of the tree, spread over about six months.

Now in his workshop stands another piece, this one a Chippendale chest-on-chest, six spaces for drawers on the top, six for drawers on the bottom. It stands about 7 feet high. The walnut sides and the butternut tops and bottoms of each chest are dovetailed together, and the maple drawer runners are installed. He has cut out a triangular piece that will become the pediment top and veneered it with black walnut limb wood so that the grain of each side opens toward the center of the triangle. The unstained wood is light brown and is slightly redolent of black walnuts. The undecorated edges are sharp and clean, the angles square and true. He has put it aside for the summer, as he always does, so that he can pursue one of his other passions, fly-fishing for trout and salmon.

Three of Howard's relatives are full-time antique dealers, and his grandmother's brother made violins. Howard is an eighth generation native of Schoharie County, as well as a historian and genealogist. He is as familiar with the early history of his family as he is with the early history of the region: The Bartholomews were French Huguenots who, after the repeal of the Edict of Nantes in 1685, fled first to Switzerland, then to Holland, where many became Dutch Reformed. In the early eighteenth century, they fled to New Jersey, and then, in 1715, four brothers came to Schoharie County and settled. Schoharie County lies along the north slope of the Catskills and was settled somewhat earlier than the rest of the Catskills. It forms a kind of buffer between the Catskills and the Mohawk Valley, which is more accessible than the Catskills, more industrialized, more prosperous, and perhaps, more sophisticated. Sherrie Batholomew (née Nesbit), who was born and raised in Delaware County, views the old folks back home (some 30 miles away) as a little rusticated compared to the folks in Schoharie County. Her ancestry in the region, Scottish by nationality, goes back nearly as far as Howard's, and Howard is quick to point out the origins of the settlement of Delaware County in the mid-eighteenth century. Scottish crofters were forced off the land they had traditionally farmed in Scotland by the passage of the Enclosure Acts (which allowed the fencing in of the landlord's pasturage, and the exclusion of all livestock but the master's). They came to America and sought good sheep-raising land, which was to be found in the Catskills. They were poor though, and the hilly, cool, inaccessible valleys of Delaware County were less desirable, and therefore less expensive, than the already settled land in Ulster, Sullivan, Schoharie, and Orange counties, not to mention Dutchess and Columbia counties, across the Hudson. The names bespeak the nationalities of the settlers: More desirable land went earlier, to Dutch homesteaders and patroons. The Scotch-Irish came next. The counties with Indian names were the last to be claimed.

Howard, through his uncles and through his own collecting, is aware of what sort of furniture can still be found in the area—painted blanket trunks brought by Dutch settlers, and a few Queen Anne pieces, but almost no Windsor chairs, for example, because those people who owned such chairs simply didn't come to the area. Those who did get there, however, developed their own styles of furniture making, which differed from what they had left behind. American Chippendale grew out of English Chippendale, but is simpler, less likely to be ornately painted, more likely to use the varieties of native wood for decorative purposes. Maple, especially, develops various diseases that give it well-defined patterns in the grain that shine out from the natural bright yellow color of the wood. A lot of maple, which is very hard and rather difficult to work with, is used for drawer fronts. Less showy maple is used for drawer runners, because friction doesn't damage it. It was Howard's appreciation of antiques that got him into furniture making—he realized that there were a number of pieces that were not available in the area, or were too expensive for his budget, and so he

© Michael Owen

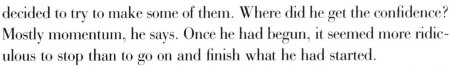

decided to try to make some of them. Where did he get the confidence? Mostly momentum, he says. Once he had begun, it seemed more ridiculous to stop than to go on and finish what he had started.

Once he had made the first chest, from plans he sent away for, the die was cast and other pieces followed, each demanding particular tools, new techniques, more refined skills. Now, after eight years, he has made twenty-five pieces, some for friends and relatives as well as for his own household. In the spring of 1987, after twenty years teaching history, he intends to take another step that calls for great self-confidence—he is going to retire from teaching and go into furniture making full time. He has gathered together some 5,500 board feet of hardwood of all kinds, including a lot of black walnut. Much of this he gets for free or for a nominal sum, for cutting it down and hauling it away. His market will be collectors of fine furniture, and he thinks that his overhead will be low enough so that he can compete with major furniture makers. He has already set himself an hourly wage that reflects, he thinks, his level of experience: He is experienced enough to know what he is doing, but inexperienced enough to have to be careful.

Meanwhile, it is high summer. The Bartholomews spend much of their time at their summer place, in a different world, as they say, but a world only 12 miles south, on Route 30, of the world of work. The flood plain of Schoharie Creek, which rises on the slopes of Indian Head Mountain, not far from Woodstock and only 10 miles from the Hudson River, and runs northwest and then north to the Mohawk, which flows into the Hudson, is, at Middleburgh, wide and fertile. The low-lying land has deeper topsoil and a warmer microclimate than much of the Catskills, and Howard grows a veritable truck farm of vegetable and fruit crops: The orchard contains apples, pears, peaches, plums, and the garden is ripening tomatoes and pumpkins and peppers and potatoes and corn and sunflowers. The house is the oldest inhabited building in Schoharie County and dates from the mid-eighteenth century. The creek is clean enough to swim in and to drink from, wild enough to be full of bass, whitefish, trout. Howard and Alex take the boat out and fish nearly every evening.

The difference between the two worlds is not in their relative orderliness. Just as everything in Middleburgh has its place, here, the grass is mowed, the garden neatly mulched, and the fruit trees pruned. Each is devoted to the realization of a different ideal, though. Inside the house in Middleburgh, the atmosphere is urbane and sophisticated. The carpets are Oriental—richly colored, ornately figured, bespeaking the influences of other lands, in the same way that the decorations of Chippendale furniture took their inspiration from trade with the East. The walls are covered with paintings and books—the tools and fittings of culture and education. Here at the country house, a finely finished Chippendale lowboy would be out of place, overdressed. This ideal, also an ideal of the eighteenth century, is the ideal of the well-tended garden, the simple life, the harmonious clockworks of the natural world. The man is at home in his garden, knowledgeable about plants and trees, frugal in his use of them. Howard, digging potatoes after splitting firewood, seems to realize as a kind of genetic endowment the whole early history of the region and of his family. He puts the potatoes in a bag and then into my car, generously, as if sending them, it seems to me, rocketing into the much more profligate and much less orderly future.

© Jonathan Postma

# Rosemarie Torre

The artist is surrounded by the accoutrements of his art: He stands at the easel, palette in hand, just happening to glance toward the viewer. He is dark, with a dark beard and piercing black eyes. He wears a smock, but under it, he is perfectly turned out in a tweed suit. The model hides modestly behind an ornately painted French screen, just her face and her bare arm showing. All about, in careless disorder, lie paintings and paints. The windows at the back of the room open onto the garden, and it is a sunny day in May or June; the garden is colorful with flowers. He is a wealthy dilettante, or perhaps he is the successful book illustrator of Henry James's story, "The Real Thing." He has the cozy, prosperous, Tory air of the English Edwardian period. To furnish his studio, he has chosen an elegant selection of chinoiserie—desk with chair, a daybed, a tall curio cabinet, the screen, a table. All is black lacquer, hand-painted in intricate Oriental scenes with gold and other bright colors. He and his model both have the sort of porcelain complexions that will never age, because they are porcelain, and only one-twelfth normal size. The studio they stand in was designed, built, and painted by Rosemarie Torre, though they themselves were modeled and clothed by a friend of Rosemarie's who specializes in custom-designed porcelain miniature figures.

Or perhaps the painter is Rosemarie's father, the German painter Erich Schraeger, or his father, who was a painter, too. At any rate it is a safe and alluring scene. There are others: an Edwardian bedroom, all done in pink ruffles. The baby plays in his cradle while the four-year-old is discovered by the mother to have been using her watercolors on the table as well as on the paper she was given. A large four-poster forms the centerpiece of the furnishings; an imposing armoire stands against the wall. Everything is country French, feminine, ruffled, and deeply upholstered.

A more sinister piece, in a distinctly Chinese setting, is the voluptuously fuchsia "opium bed": The curtains are drawn back for now, revealing the brilliant interior, but that won't last long—everything about this bed is made for secrecy. And what is going on behind the shining black circular screen, on which two ladies in kimonos approach a beautiful temple, conversing and enjoying the flowering trees and shrubs all about them?

Rosemarie is used to oohs and ahs. She has been making dollhouses and miniatures for almost thirty years, ever since she made her first dollhouse for her son, Andreas. She oohs and ahs herself over pieces she has seen at shows or has bought: the sterling silver tea set, a reproduction of an English Victorian tea set, tiny but heavy; Chippendale secretaries with hidden drawers; a Bombay chest made by a friend in which the hand-carved sides curve vertically as well as horizontally and match perfectly; petit point Oriental carpets so finely stitched that at first glance they look printed. She says, "I don't think there is anything nobody makes. And if there is, then if somebody wants it, somebody's going to make it. What there is in large, you can find in miniature. They make music instruments which play, harpsichords, stringed instruments. They make guns, farm implements. Anything." It is hard to be immune to the worlds created—in their very tininess they seem safe and peaceful.

Rosemarie Torre's world has not always been safe or peaceful by any means. She was born in Dresden before World War II, and at the age of five moved to the Erz-Gebirge Mountains. At thirteen she returned to the Dresden that had been leveled by Allied bombing and taken over by the Russians. "When the Russians came in we went back with the retreating German army to Czechoslovakia, but then we ended up in Dresden again. We had to walk through the whole of Czechoslovakia.

"The rumor would start, the Russians are coming, and so everyone abandoned their vehicles and ran for the hills. Naturally nothing happened. But you couldn't find anymore your truck, so you just sort of walked it. That was the only time I was scared in all my life. It was a little country road, and we were walking on the side to make room for the tanks to move in, but they didn't stop. They had orders to keep going. It was a very eerie feeling, you know. We had just gotten my father out of the hospital, because he had had a motorcycle accident, so he had broken a hip, but he had to walk for days. There was a bridge, and there was a rumor that everybody who was on this side was going to be put in a labor camp, and the bridge is dynamited, it's going to blow up, but we said, 'no labor camp,' so we sneaked over the bridge, we were the only ones; we didn't know if this bridge was going to go up any second. But you come to a point, you don't care. So we went over that bridge, and we stayed the night down right underneath the bridge, on the bank of the river, and the bombs were dropping here and there, and we just went to bed, we were so tired, to heck what happened. The next day we went on the road again, and outside town we met the

Russians coming in. Both of my grandparents were there in Dresden, so we stayed with them until we decided then to leave East Germany. We were from the suburbs, and there were still things standing at the end of the war."

She goes on. "Luckily in our whole family there was only one family that got killed by the bombs, my mother's stepbrother and his wife and child. Outside of this we were very lucky. They were all in Russia in the war, but they all came back, surprisingly. Except my father, after the war, they took him to Russia to a labor camp. For five years he was over there. They took lots of skilled men. Then Stalin had the amnesty and they all went home again, what was left of them. My father, they found out he could paint, so he was painting pictures for them— mostly bear scenes. He said all he was painting was woods and teddy bears. But it was very primitive—he had to make his own paints."

In 1952, Rosemarie and her family left East Germany for West Germany, then spent 1953 in Canada. In 1954, they came to the United States. In Europe, Erich Schraeger worked as an art restorer, repairing and reclaiming frescoes in churches, among other things. He continued this work in the States, doing gilding work at the Metropolitan, working for Onassis, for the Rockefellers. Rosemarie has a picture of him working on the Blue Room restoration in the White House. She says, "I miss him. He was very handy. I tell you, I must have had the only electric kitchen when I was a child. Electric stove, running water, lights. It sticks in the family. In Long Island, the Westbury Gardens, they had silk wallpaper. On lots of things I worked with him at home, because he would bring the silk home and paint the wallpaper on the silk, and then they put it on the walls."

Rosemarie went for a while to the Kunsthochschule in Dresden but didn't have a chance to take a degree before she left for the west. In America, one of her first jobs was designing jacquard neckties for a one-man necktie operation. Later, she got into textile design, first for a company, then free lance. But the introduction of textiles from the Far

East and India ended the free lance textile design business. She switched to miniatures: "I had a friend who went to a miniature show, and she said, 'They had a bed they sold for sixty dollars, a couch.' I said, 'You've got to be kidding. Who would pay so much money for it?' So I sent for a contract, and they sent me one for the next show, and that's the way it started."

Her pieces are not reproductions. She takes ideas from period pieces, but then she designs them herself. She makes desks and chairs and armoires and a number of styles of screens, as well as pie crust tables, trunks, tea chests, chests of drawers, revolving fans, sewing boxes, settees, four-poster beds, opium beds, vanities, lap secretaries, upholstered couches and armchairs, and just about anything else that strikes her fancy. Though she has five or six dollhouses that she has made, she prefers the freedom of building single rooms. The pieces of furniture range in price from about $35 to $790, from a small sewing box with scenes painted on the outside, to the large, intricate armoires, painted all over, inside and out, front and back, with a variety of scenes and figures. The pieces are beautifully shaped and thought out, but it is the painting that catches the eye—the lines are impossibly fine, and the figures impossibly detailed with tiny expressions on their tiny faces. The screens deserve the same sort of lengthy regard as their full-sized counterparts might, and Rosemarie aims for that—every scene is different, and she is always looking for new ideas.

Now she lives on Old River Road, between Margaretville and Roxbury. With her husband, a retired composer, she runs a bed and breakfast called The Miniature Dollhouse Museum. It is a long white house that stands under the brow of a stony Catskill hillside, surrounded by lawns and flowers. The dollhouse museum, along with Rosemarie's shop, are in what used to be the garage. The workshop where she builds her pieces is behind the shop. The second workshop, where she paints and upholsters her pieces, is on the third floor, just off the bedroom. The woodworking tools are built just like any woodworker's tools, except that they are table size. She has a workshop full—a miniature bench saw, a miniature bandsaw, a miniature router, a miniature lathe, two miniature sanders. She cuts her pieces by hand out of basswood, birch plywood, or maple. The most difficult task is cutting the cabriole chair legs. "Some days you cut them out without effort and other days, you just have to throw out one after the other. Sometimes it's the wood, too. Wood is not always the same. Some days it's too hard and some days it's too soft." If there are turned legs, she turns them, and if there is routing (decorative grooves), she does the

© Jonathan Postma

routing. "Scale" means 1 foot to 1 inch, and a premium is placed on exactitude of scale, so that the thickness of the pieces, after they have been decorated, is as important as their length and width. The legs and backs and seats are put together with yellow Elmer's glue, and then the real work begins.

Miniature makers who make stained furniture stain before they glue, because stain will not take over glue. Fits must be especially exact, then. She says, "Since I paint, I can always fill in or just take off a little bit. I don't have to worry about glue, because it's going to be painted anyway. Once I put the sealer on, about two coats, to seal the porousness of the wood, then I sand it again, then I spray paint it quite a few coats. In between, I sand it again, and then it is ready for decorating. I use the regular flat paint from paint stores." The sanding is intended to remove all traces of wood grain from the surface, because Rosemarie prefers an absolutely smooth base. Such tiny painting would be marred by any roughness.

How long does it take to make a piece? She says, "Spray painting only takes a minute. But then you have to wait till it dries, in the meantime, you do something else, then you go back to doing this, then you go back to something else. You work on a lot of pieces at a time, so it's hard to tell. Actually, it takes longest to get the base coats on, because with all the sanding, sometimes you think you've got it, and then you see the wood grain again, and you have to start all over, sanding it down and starting all over again painting. That takes a long time to get the right base. At the end, I like to have a nice smooth finish on it, like ivory."

She paints in watercolor, and two designs are never alike. She gets her ideas from art books, and especially relies on a two-volume set of illustrations of furniture from Italy. She says, "I paid two hundred fifty dollars for these two books and had to wait a year to get them. A book finder had to get them for me, but I wanted them! There's découpage in them, and all hand-painted furniture. They are really some books! I get a lot of ideas out of them, and wherever else I can pick something up." The watercolors can cling only to the surface of the flat paint, so to achieve the glossy look of authentic lacquer, Rosemarie applies a coat of sealer and lacquer after painting on the pictures. The sealer simultaneously gives her the look she wants and preserves the painting she has done. After the sealer and lacquer, she paints on the gold parts. The watercolors allow her to achieve the delicacy she needs, but in order for the colors to show against the black background, she has to put on many coats, which takes a good deal of time.

The secret of her precise, fine painting is the brushes she uses, which are imported French sable brushes. She says, "I use the same brush I used to use for my textiles, a French quill they call it, and they are very hard to come by. As a matter of fact, there's only one place in the city I get it, and the last time I bought three because they hardly had any left, and they said there's no craftsmen to make the brushes anymore. They must use a special hair from the sable, because when you press them down, they don't flatten out. Most brushes, even the ones that call themselves sable, you put them down, and they spread their feet out. This is a heavy brush, but it has a point, it comes down to a hairline. It's not one or two hairs, it's more, but they stay. They can last you for years, if you take care of them, but sometimes you forget—the phone rings, and you put them so that the point twists. Forget it. You'll never get the point straight again. Oh, I could shoot myself when that happens. Once that point is twisted, there is no way."

Finally, she does the upholstery, which is tiny and complex. The cushions are glued rather than sewn, except for the tufting, which is made with hand stitches. She stuffs the cushions with quilt batting, or with layers of spongy antistatic dryer sheets cut to size. The cushions are pleated and piped, have square, neat corners, and look comfortable.

Rosemarie depends on her craft for her living, which means that she goes to a number of miniature shows each year. Miniatures have been popular for about twenty-five years, since before Rosemarie began. The audience miniature craftsmen aim for is collectors—these aren't doll furniture, but more like alternative lives. Miniature collecting seems to be enough of a passion for enough people to support more than a few miniature craftsmen. At the last convention of the National Association of Miniature Enthusiasts, over 100 craftspersons displayed their wares to over 1,500 members. The show runs for four days, and is only open to the public on the last day. This year it is in Chicago. Rosemarie gets most of her supplies at this show and likes to go so that she can see the latest innovations. For example, not long ago she found a new kind of brass furniture hardware that a craftswoman from New York had begun making with a photoengraving method, much finer and closer to scale, as well as much more ornate than hardware previously available. It is solid brass, but thinner than paper, tiny drawer pulls and hinges and ornamental fixtures.

The shows are fun but chancy. Rosemarie likes to sell most of her work outright, which allows her to try out new designs, but also means that she must have a lot of pieces ready for the show—at least fifty. Sometimes, as happened two years ago in Rochester, at the opening of the Margaret Woodbury Strong Museum (a museum of dolls and miniatures), she sells everything. Last year in Cincinnati, sales were disappointing, and as recently as this past spring, Rosemarie was thinking of getting out of the business. "It looked like the old collectors all had their collections full, and the younger ones weren't so much interested; but now, if the trend holds up, maybe the business is picking up again. It's mostly elderly people. A lot of doctors' wives. There's somebody, a man, who has somebody go around to all the top shows and buy things up. I think he is starting a museum somewhere." There are a number of museums.

She is philosophical about the ups and downs of the shows. "If something sells good, I'll keep it for a while. Eventually, you can tell. It fizzles out. Even if you go to a different part of the country. Why, I

don't know. I say, 'These people haven't seen it.' But all the people have the same idea. A couple of years they go in for this and a couple of years they go in for that. How they get the message, I don't know." And it depends on price. The small sewing boxes, $45, and the small painted mirrors, $30, are consistent sellers to collectors who say, "I simply must have a piece of yours." Not everyone can afford the French armoires, $790, and the small, many-drawered spice chests for the same price. The work of other craftsmen can be much more expensive—the Chippendale secretaire that Rosemarie likes so much is $2,000; the petit point rugs in silk thread command $1,000 or more. But one of these pieces may take 4 or 5 months to complete. "So how many of those can you make in a year?" She shrugs.

Until August 1984, Rosemarie and her husband lived in Syosset, Long Island. The move to the Catskills was an old wish of Rosemarie's, although her husband, a typesetter and compositor for a printing concern that printed in every language in the world, was a born city man. The owner of his company died, however, and the son was not especially interested in continuing the business, so Mr. Torre retired. She says, "In Syosset, we lived for twenty-four years in the same neighborhood. I never went by the neighbors', and went into the next house, or talked to the one across the street. You know, everybody worked, was in a hurry, everybody minded their own business. Here, it's entirely different. People are friendly, say hello, good morning, hold the door for you. Down there, you get it smashed in your face. I talk to more people here than I ever did in Long Island in twenty-four years. I like the city, I like to dress up, but I am a country type. I like to get back to the country." Now, they run a bed and breakfast, though actually, Rosemarie would like to be running a small inn. She house-hunted for years, while trying to persuade her husband to leave the city, and then, while trying to sell the Syosset house. She says, "It used to be a standing joke. Oh, here she comes, here comes the decorator again, because every house I went in, I redecorated, you know."

The house has many rooms for Rosemarie to decorate, and she is slowly getting all of them just the way she wants them. Two years ago she remodeled the kitchen, designing everything and doing most of the work. Much of the furniture she has either built or refinished herself, and most of the paintings and decorations on the walls are hers, though a few were done by her father. The gardens, she asserts, were a mess— overgrown, beds almost nonexistent. Now they spill down the hillside in front of the house, a profusion of color. The spot is quiet, the house sheltered by a low hill in the back. It is a world that is safe and peaceful.

# Steve Heller and Martha Frankel

The furniture Steve Heller makes at Fabulous Furniture, on Route 28 in Boiceville, has evolved into what might be considered a perfect expression of the natural Catskill world, and in fact, he calls his store Mother Nature's Furniture Store. Unlike many local furniture builders and carpenters, he uses only local wood for his pieces, and he specializes in varieties of maple, especially spalted maple—maple that has been discolored and misshapen by a particular disease so that it is scored in interesting patterns with short black lines. He also likes to use black walnut, black cherry, and butternut. He does not buy lumber, he buys trees, and he has connections with all of the local lumbering operations, so that when they come across a tree he might like, they give him a call. He then cuts down the tree himself and carries it home, where it may sit for a number of years before he makes up his mind to use it. There is nothing he likes more than a deformed maple three feet in diameter with decided crotches.

He says, "Now I know all the loggers. They get a new woodlot. I go and I walk the woodlot, decide which trees that I want, cut them down, pull them out. You can always tell there's something with the tree, but there's certain things you can't tell till you saw it open. Then you know for sure. You can say, boy, that's definitely curly maple, but you never really know till you saw it. Maple's real funny. All these weird things happen to maple. Nobody knows why. It becomes curly, it becomes bird's eye, it becomes blistered, it becomes spalted. There are signs that it's been deformed, but they don't always prove true. One time I walked four hundred acres and picked six trees, and that was from literally thousands of trees. We don't use oak. You know, a three-foot or four-foot oak has basically the same grain as an eighteen-inch oak tree. We don't use oak, pine, ash, poplar, because the grain is very straight and plain compared to maple or walnut or cherry, so why fool with that stuff? Part of our whole trip is that I want somebody to say, My God, what kind of weird wood is this?"

Some years ago, he took a black walnut tree from the Bard College grounds across the river, which he estimates to have been 300 or 400 years old. When he brought it home, he wasn't sure what he wanted to do with it—it was too incredible even to saw into boards. The solution came from someone who had heard of him through a friend. He says, "I thought it was a crank call. Somebody calls me up one day and says, 'We want a black walnut mantlepiece three feet wide, six feet long, and eight inches thick.' That's unheard of, to be able to get a piece of wood that big. But we had it. It was great." From the rest of the log, he made some desks and tables, and there are still some pieces left of it. Steve expects to be able to use all of the wood for something, at least the chopping boards and mirrors that sell inexpensively in the shop.

The next step is sawing and drying, both of which are more difficult with the sort of wood Heller uses. In the first place, a tree when it's first cut down contains 70 percent moisture. The air of the average home contains about 10 to 12 percent moisture, which means that as a piece of furniture releases its moisture into the air it might crack ("check") or warp. He says, "You can't go and buy this lumber anyplace. We try to air dry it for a year. Lumberyards would consider this low-grade or novelty lumber. A lumber company couldn't do this on a production basis, because there would be too much spoilage. We want to dry the wood as slowly as possible." After a year outside, he sends it to a local kiln, where the moisture content is reduced from 20 percent ("No matter how many years you air dry it anyplace, it won't go below twenty percent") to 6 or 7 percent. Steve is proud of the fact that though his shop produces hundreds of pieces of furniture, there are no returns. This he attributes to the care they take in drying the wood.

Steve is in his early forties, short and wiry, wearing a Fabulous Furniture T-shirt with the sleeves and collar cut off. His black curly hair is about collar length, pushed behind his ears. His long beard is shot with a few threads of gray. His manner is intensely hearty and his gaze ready and direct. His partner, Martha Frankel, who runs the showroom, doesn't work in the shop but spends a good deal of time finishing mirrors, screwing in hanging wires, and answering the telephone. Martha, blonde, in her late thirties, is about as warm as a person could be, and the showroom is bright and welcoming. The phone rings a lot and friends are in and out. Martha and Steve are happy to hear from everyone.

The showroom contains about forty tables, and they have a characteristic style. The tops are thick and irregularly shaped, their outlines following the original shape of the tree. Often there is a hole in the middle of the table, where the two "book-matched" pieces diverge, and this hole is fitted with a piece of glass cut exactly to shape. On some of the tables, the outside edges are still covered with bark, and on most of them the variation in color between the sapwood and the heart wood is used to give an even stronger sense of the natural shape of the wood.

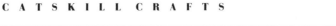

It is obvious that these tables are former trees. The bases are as thick as the tops, made of the same sort of wood and in the same style. The finish is so shiny and smooth that, to both hand and eye, it seems continuous with the glass insert. It is also, Steve says, indestructible, part penetrating oil and part polyurethane. It is a paradoxical sort of high tech finish that encourages one to gaze at the wood and touch it and appreciate it. Two coffee tables, in fact, made of dyed curly maple, have signs on them asking people not to touch them. Martha says that she was forced to put these signs on these tables, not because they are more delicate than the others, but because the finish is so remarkably shiny that people were knocking their rings on it to see how hard it was. Another style of table has an even more organic and sculptural feel to it. These are highly finished but roughly shaped pedestal bases fitted with glass tops. There are about three of these, plus numerous smaller pieces: clocks, shelves, sculptures, cutting boards. Nothing goes to waste.

And it is impossible to overlook Steve's latest idea, the front end of a 1957 Cadillac, aquamarine, headlights lit, 1957 license plate. It is a bar. He says, "I'm a motorhead, too, you know." He has also made stereo cabinets and other pieces of furniture out of front and back ends of fifties Cadillacs—only Cadillacs. One of his sheds, back by the shop, contains three whole Cadillac bodies by Fisher, sliced up and ready to be fitted out for some client's living room.

The business presses at the boundaries of the Fabulous Furniture lot. Steve's assistant lives behind the showroom, and the area around the workshop is stacked with raw materials in various stages; around the driveway, fat gray logs lie waiting to be sawed into lumber. Pine to the east, walnut to the west, maple back by the shop. A spot that looks to be full of abandoned sheet metal is actually the place where the cutting is done, and the sheets of metal are covering partly sawed-up logs and protecting them from the weather. The junked schoolbus and the metal truck bodies turn out to be wood preserving rooms—airtight and hot, even in the winter, so that the wood is always dry and always "cooking," as Steve says, not soaking up humidity and swelling. After it comes back from the kiln, he is able to maintain it at 7 percent moisture content indefinitely. The schoolbus contains smaller pieces of fragrant black walnut, waiting to be made into bases for tables. Out of one truck box rolls the intoxicating odor of red cedar, also local. Even the maple smells, though not as strongly as the others, and Steve mentions the characteristic sweet smell of cherry when he works with that.

When Steve first started making furniture sixteen years ago, he made it out of slabwood that he got from local sawmills. The slabwood is what the sawmill cuts away to square off the log before cutting it into boards. His workshop was so small that he couldn't actually work in it—he could only store his tools and his wood there. When he wanted to work, he would take everything outside, and when it began to rain, not infrequent in the Catskills, he would rush to carry everything in again. He wasn't able to make a living from his work, but it intrigued him, and somehow he got through. Finally he came to buy the present property in Boiceville. He used to have a shop at Winchell's Corners, in Shokan, but, he says, "I'd been there for two years, and I was still borrowing money on a pretty regular basis to make it. Then I saw that this place was for sale, and it was totally fucked up. I'm sure he was the only guy ever to lose money on Catskill property. He had this property for ten years in the Catskills, and he sold it for less than he paid for it. Everything got worse, really run down. So I made a deal with my pop that I'd buy it and renovate it and move the business over here, and if in a year or so it didn't go well, we could sell the property and I would pay him back." Steve's father was sympathetic partly because he is himself an artist and sculptor in Woodstock.

The place used to be a Catskill motel, and the showroom was the manager's office and living quarters. What had once been the row of cabins became, over the course of about six years, the woodworking shop, 12 feet deep and 70 feet long, all the cabins joined bit by bit into

a drafty, inefficient, but inexpensive working area, heated by a number
of woodstoves. Steve and Martha were just beginning to feel that they
were really making it—Steve had a full line of tools and methods that
he was confident in, they were doing good business, and their assistant,
hired six months before, was settling in and beginning to take over the
production side of the work so that Steve could concentrate on designing. Then, the day before Halloween in 1978, when Martha was in
Woodstock and Steve was down the road, one of the woodstoves apparently sparked and set the workshop on fire. By the time Keith Johnson,
a friend who was passing on Route 28, happened to see the fire, the
entire shop, uninsured, and all the machinery had been destroyed. The
showroom and the living quarters were untouched, luckily, but everything else was lost. Steve says, "I had just finished working seven years,
twenty hours a day, seven days a week, and I didn't think I had it in
me to do it again. I remember sitting on the old deck there, and just
freaking out. And a neighbor came by who we didn't know well, and
she brought us something, some money or food. It was unbelievable
how the town supported us. Some friends organized a benefit, and they
raised something like three grand for us. That's why we have that sign
up there, The Shop That Friends Built. Every weekend, fifty people
showed up and worked for free." They bulldozed away the old place,
put up the present concrete block building in the dead of winter, found
used replacement machines in hundreds of places. Within four months,
they were back in business.

Martha is candid about the effects of the fire, both positive and
negative. She thinks it took them much longer to recover, psychologi-
cally, than they expected. For at least two years, they suffered from lots
of anxiety, isolation, and depression, and for a long time after that, they
couldn't be away from the shop without compelling fears about what
might be going on in their absence. "I can't count the number of
movies we've left before the end," she says. But even so, the result of
the fire was to remake their life in a good way—the new shop was

designed and built to be a woodworking shop—it is larger and airier than the old place, warmer in the winter, cooler in the summer, easier to keep clean, less dangerous, less likely to burn, even with all the sawdust and wood that must inevitably accumulate. It is insured. It is built to accommodate the sort of processes Steve has made his trademark. They also no longer live behind the showroom, but instead on twenty-five acres back in the woods in West Shokan.

The shop is spacious and bright, with big windows and a big garage door. Barrels of sawdust and shavings stand everywhere. In the drying room, two tabletops shine in the heat. One is for a Japanese-style dining table, done on commission, and the other is for a coffee table to go into the showroom. About half of Fabulous Furniture's work is done on commission for steady customers or people who have heard of the shop by word of mouth. The style of the furniture is so distinct, and each piece is so unique that no one is ever going to begin to suggest that you

© Michael Owen

might find something similar in the Sears catalogue. There is also nothing in the least subtle about any of the pieces. Even jammed together in the showroom, each one announces itself like a piece of sculpture and asks to be looked at, top and bottom, like a sculpture. And yet the forms and the colors, dictated by the shape of the trees, are natural and comforting, recognizable after a moment, familiar after another moment. They could easily be introduced into almost any room, even a Laura Ashley flounce-and-print sort of decorating scheme.

This sculptural quality is something that Steve finds in the pieces of wood he keeps. The design of the piece does not precede the making of it, as it does with Howard Bartholomew, for example. Instead, he goes to the wood bins seeking something and sometimes he doesn't find it. He says, "We look through all the wood to find the right pieces for the right shape, size, feeling. We do that a lot. Sometimes we go through the piles of wood ten times, start out in one building, go through, come back. Not find anything, and finally it hits us. And also, my eye is always looking for the piece that will make the right coffee table with the piece of glass in it."

When he does find it, he follows specific techniques that he has worked out for specific purposes. He likes "book-matched" pieces—that is, pieces where a thick board with a strongly marked grain is sliced into two boards, which are then put together side by side, so that the grain forms an interesting symmetrical pattern. The sides are always glued, without dowels, which Steve feels weaken the joint ("It never breaks at the joint," Martha says. "If it breaks, it always breaks somewhere else.") and usually without splining (a process where the surface is grooved with a router and then fitted with a strip of wood that is glued to a matching groove on the adjoining surface) unless the curve in the wood is such that the end-grain of each piece is coming together. The goal is strength as well as beauty. The bases are doweled together, and then the tops are attached to the bases with screws, the only metal in the work. Steve used to dowel the bases to the tops, but preferred the convenience of being able to remove the top if something came back for refinishing.

The finishes are startlingly shiny and nearly indestructible. On most pieces, Steve uses no stains. The walnut furniture is rather pale, the maple bright yellow, the cherry more tan than red. The logs distributed in piles about the yard are uniformly weathered to a neutral gray, the natural color of wood exposed to wind and rain. It is inside the showroom that the real color of the wood is revealed, and then preserved under twenty coats of tung oil and polyurethane, applied and sanded, applied and sanded. The result of Steve's methods, time, and labor is to encourage the viewer to contemplate the wood itself, its shape, color, and grain, as it might be in the forest, but, of course, isn't.

Is it his first love? He is dismissive. Probably not, though he has seriously considered getting out of the business only once since the fire, when he was discouraged by the hassles of hiring and training employees, doing paperwork. He says, "It's incredible the physical space, the volume of material, and the machinery you need to do it correctly. The capital investment is ridiculous compared to the return on it. It's hard." From the top step of the shop, the buildings and truck boxes and wood piles spread out in two arms. The two arms embrace that smaller shed as if that were his first love, the 8 × 8 shed that contains those four Cadillac bodies that have been sawed apart and stacked together. When I ask to see inside, his normal, self-effacing, relaxed attitude gives way to enthusiasm. He unlocks and opens the door. The light is dim, but sufficient for me to appreciate the optical illusion of all those cars, those bumpers and headlights and assertive fenders and massive fins contained, confined, concentrated. No engines, no roofs or seats or tires, but they still seem to be coming and going. They are pink and turquoise and red and white, unnatural colors, unlike the wood Steve uses in every way except one, and that is the way in which they will be allowed, someday, to assert their own natures, enhanced by art but not transformed.

© Jonathan Postma

# Laura Wilensky and Henry Cavanagh

Laura Wilensky and Henry Cavanagh are ceramists who live in Lomontville, in Ulster County. Both went to art school at SUNY New Paltz, and both live by selling their work through galleries and crafts shows. They speak eloquently about the important concerns of potters and other craftspeople in the 1980s. What follows is an abridged and clarified version of an interview conducted on July 28, 1986.

JS: What kind of kilns do you have?

LW: Electric.

JS: How come you have electric instead of gas?

HC: Laura's the technician.

LW: For the colors that we use, the electric kiln provides what's called an oxidation atmosphere that's very clean, and you get a wide range of colors.

HC: And consistent predictable performance.

LW: You'll get the same results every time.

JS: Do you have one kiln or—

LW: We have three. One of them is a small test kiln that can't go up to the full range but is used for quick low-firing. The others are used for the whole process. We do three firings. The first is the bisque, where you just harden the piece so that you can apply some of the colors or glazes. Then the second firing is the glaze firing. All mine are fired to about 2,400 degrees for the glaze and some of the background stains, and Henry does that for his hippos; his hippos are high-fired with stains, minimal glazes.

JS: Do you do the painting after?

HC: Yeah. There are two types of painting. One is water-base staining that Laura mentioned, which is under the glaze; it's called an underglaze. When the piece has been fired to bisque and it's bone dry and very absorbent, then you brush this stain onto it, and it picks up the slight indentations. This "curtain effect" is more real-looking than if I painted it on, and it's less work. After you fire the glaze on, then you come back and you china paint the brighter colors. The glaze and the stains are applied and fired to 2,400 degrees. The china paints are much more delicate, and they only go up to about 1,200 or 1,300 degrees.

LW: And they're very precise. They'll stay pretty much where you put them, and the colors are pretty much unchanged.

HC: Here is a piece with stain. This filmy effect is under the glaze, and it would be almost impossible to get with the china paints, which kind of lay on the top.

LW: They sit on the surface, they don't really blend in, whereas the stains really soak into the clay and become part of it .

JS: Is that what you do for the hippos, Henry?

HC: It's basically the same process, but I do less of it. Laura is dealing with a cup as a canvas, and she paints onto it, and that's important to her. When you're dealing with three-dimensional objects, the action of the object really carries a lot of information. This sofa is stained, because I know it will give me a certain look, but this garish gold on the hooves can only be achieved with the china paints, and the silver as well. These other colors probably could have been used as a stain or a china paint, but I wanted an even application, not a watery or painterly effect, and so for that I used a china paint, which goes on more smoothly.

JS: How about for the shiny black hooves?

HC: I could have painted on a black stain and a glaze, but if the black wasn't rich enough, I couldn't really amend it, except with china paints, so I said, to hell with that, I'll just do the china paints, because I wanted a real rich black.

JS: So you evolved your techniques for knowing what you wanted to do with all these things some years ago, right?

HC: Somewhat trial and error. Here is a failed piece. [He points to a hippo at the beach, in swimming trunks.] This poor guy, I only did it two or three years ago, and you would think that after six or seven years of working in the medium, I'd have learned more. Even to the untrained eye, the colors are too dark, too mottled, there's not enough contrast, it's not bright enough or alive enough. I saw that happening, and I couldn't stop it, because once you start on a darker palette, you can only get darker, and I was trapped. [He picks up the hippo and the horse.] These guys go together, and this is their couch. This has no real reason at all, but the title of the piece is *Cookies at Fritz's Place.*

JS: What was the reaction to *Cookies at Fritz's Place* at the crafts show [The American Crafts Council Show in Springfield, Massachusetts]?

HC: It was sold. I have to assemble it now. And it was sold at a ridiculously low price, $400, which is maybe half of what it would get at a gallery. But it was sold to a collector who's assembling what may be an important collection. I was relieved. It's such an eccentric piece that I was actually relieved somebody bought it. It's a mythical meeting between Benjamin Franklin and Frederick the Great of Prussia. Frederick the Great cultivated the great minds of his time, Rousseau and Molière, and others. Franklin, I think, would have fit in, but they never met. I think Frederick would have liked Franklin. He was a great admirer of philosophers. He's still affectionately called Onkel Fritz in Germany.

JS: I take it you get a lot of inspiration from history and literature.

HC: I do.

LW: He's a real history buff.

HC: My liking of history, for instance motion picture history, made me familiar with books of stills and camera setups and scenes from movies, and when Laura was starting to do new and larger pieces where her own characters just weren't coming fast enough, I think I may have suggested that Laura look at these stills.

LW: I was using costume books as inspiration.

HC: But they were so static.

LW: The movie books have such good poses. A lot of them are over-dramatic—

HC: Rather than the fashion pose, which really is only to show you the gown and how it hangs, these are much more dramatic and they're composed better. They have got the props, they've done the research, they've put the people together in a nice configuration, and all you have to do is improve on it.

I was always a student of history, and it provides a richness of reference that the audience doesn't have to participate in or get. It's really just to keep me stimulated. I think that a piece of artwork is not really finished until it's seen, and then it's completed. Creation by the artist is just a stage in the development of the piece. And because I feel that way, I feel that what people get out of the piece identifies the piece just as much as what the artist says the piece is. So I can say that this is a mythical meeting between Benjamin Franklin and Frederick the Great, but I don't tell that to the public. It's only implied in the title, and the public doesn't need to know that. So, though the historical references are often there, it's not didactic. I'm not trying to teach history.

JS: You have those pieces, but you also do these butter dishes and teapots. Do you feel a difference? Which have you been doing longer?

HC: The hippos. And I say hippos, but I do animal figures in general. The hippos sell. They're very popular, and so for every non-hippo, I do maybe forty or fifty hippos. Although I'm capable and willing to do any other animal, I haven't hit upon other thematic material that's so popular.

JS: And so to some extent, what you do is dictated by what will sell.

HC: Yeah. I knew a farmer once who grew nothing but weeds, and he went broke. There's no point in putting all your effort into something that's—

LW: Well, I've worked on some pieces in the past that I've really enjoyed doing, and it took sometimes a couple of years for them to sell, and some of them are still going around from gallery to gallery.

HC: But they're great training. Technically you learn something. You challenge yourself and push yourself.

LW: It's important to do those pieces. Those are the pieces that you really want to do, but they happen to be very time-consuming pieces. And if they don't sell, you can't always afford to keep doing them.

JS: Do you feel a conflict between money and art?

HC: No.

LW: Yes. I think when I know that I'm going to end up selling something, I have a slightly different attitude. When I first started working, before I was thinking about selling it, I did the piece totally for me. I didn't try to cut corners in any way. I didn't have to think about the fact that I might part with it. I just went all out. Once I committed myself to making my living selling my work, and making pieces over and over again, lots of pieces, I couldn't be as emotionally involved as I was initially. And it's hard to set aside time to slow down and really get into it when you're thinking about deadlines or will this sell, can I get enough money for this? If I put in another hour on this piece, can I really command the price I should get for it? So that does interfere. I would like to get to the point where I have pieces that I can kind of do that will almost do themselves, so I can have a block of time to get back to some more involved pieces. I find it very hard to shift.

JS: You can't say, well, in the morning I'm going to do this and in the afternoon, this?

LW: You just don't always feel like it.

HC: But what slops over is the talent and not the prostitution. It's hard to keep your talent from intruding into the work that you're trying to just squeeze out like sausages. It's not like, well, now I'm going to do fine art and I've got to get off these smelly clothes from whoring around earlier in the day. It's really the other way around.

JS: But you don't feel this conflict between money and art?

HC: I used to, and maybe I still feel it in a different way. When I was a student, I lavished attention on my work just like Laura did. No holds barred, twenty-four hours a day, full steam ahead. The only consideration was your performance in comparison to your classmates', impressing the teacher, getting an excellent grade, trying as many things as possible. When you deal with it from a professional point of view, you are using all you learned to make your job easier, not necessarily to show off. A good artist ought to be able to whip these things out without really getting too bogged down in emotional involvement. Perhaps the difference between fine art and crafts, aside from material distinctions, is emotion. Fine art, at its best, captures and transfers emotion. The more out of control or ego-oriented, the better. Craft is discipline. The ego submits to the dictates of the form, the function, and the material. I think my work falls between these two generalizations.

JS: Are you more or less involved in the hippos than the butter dishes? Or is it all the same?

HC: For me, demand is the motivation, and right now, the demand is on the butter dishes, partially because of the price.

JS: What's the price?

HC: The price is absurd. The retail price for some of the butter dishes is $125! Carly Simon can come into a gallery and buy three for herself and her sister and her mother, but most people can't afford it. And yet, I might sell two hundred of them a year, at $60 wholesale. I'm trying to come out with a cheaper line of butter dishes. A few years ago I said to my gallery on Madison Avenue, hey, I can do this cheaper. I can change the clay, I can cut out some of the details, and we can go for volume, and I can wholesale it to you for maybe $15 or $20 less, you could retail it for $40 less, and the guy says, yeah, but you know, my salesperson is going to take the same time to sell and wrap a $40 piece and so it's not worth it to me. And so I went ahead and did those shortcuts anyway, without changing the price, and they still sell. People are buying the idea.

JS: So if I'm looking for a Henry Cavanagh butter dish, I should look for one that was made in '75 rather than '85.

HC: Well, yeah. You can see the difference if you could see the two together. When I get $60 for this, after having spent three hours', possibly four hours' work, I'm getting $15 an hour. For the hippos, it's a lot less per hour. I always go to a show with ten or maybe fifteen hippos. There's no sense in doing a lot of them. They're somewhat redundant, so what I have is a book, and if people show any interest at all, I refer them to the book. I say, look, you're a fishmonger? Sure I can do you a hippo selling fish just as readily as I can do a hippo selling watermelon. People can say, all right, I know what I'm going to get. I see this hippo here selling carpets and I want him reading a book, so let's just take the carpet out of his hand and put a book in his hand, and the work is static to that degree. I didn't know where I was going to go with that [*Cookies at Fritz's Place*]. I had that couch, and I started building figures for it, and my intention was to do an odalisque, maybe a woman bare from the waist up, eating bonbons or something, and lounging, waiting for her lover with a cat in her lap. And it turned out to be this. Once I start, I have no control over the way things are going to go. But when I have a special order to do, a discipline takes over. I got a call early the other morning, and this guy whom I'd never heard of before saw my work, and he noticed that the highest price on any of my work at the Rhinebeck Fair was $400. He wanted two pieces, and he wanted to pay $400 each for the two pieces. My eyes began to spin. Wow, that's found money, because I've already got my next three or four months budgeted out, and I know what I can expect to make, and if I can fit this guy into the time, then that's maybe $800. And then he started describing what he wanted me to make, and my heart sank.

JS: It was real complicated?

HC: No! It was just so uninspired and stupid and trite and empty and devoid of any kind of inspiration that I said, I'm really going to have to work for this money, and this guy is not going to care. He wants to spend $800. That's his main goal. It became more and more sterile as he described it.

LW: He'll find a way. He does a lot of commissions, and they're often his best pieces, and he can be really stuck on how to approach them.

HC: But I'll earn my damned money.

JS: Can I ask you how you begin and what you do?

HC: This ceramic process is very unappealing. Because it starts with a formless lump of clay, and who knows what's in there? And through the stages, you take that lump of clay and you begin to form it, and sometimes you might just squish it around, and you have abstract shapes, then you start refining and refining that abstract shape until it becomes a recognizable reality.

JS: [Some wing chairs, dried but not bisque fired, are sitting on a nearby drying rack.] Tell me how you made that wing chair?

HC: I looked at a picture of a wing chair and I made a drawing of a wing chair as it would be broken into parts, and then I made a stencil of those individual parts, and I put the stencil on clay that I rolled out, a flat piece of clay, and I cut out the silhouette of each of the separate cushions and wings of an armchair and put them together. But at that point, I had almost a Chinese screen, just a thin piece. So then I began to build up, to form the dimensionality by adding more clay and brushing it with a wet brush so that it evened out. But I didn't know how to make this when I started.

JS: Is that cushion solid clay?

HC: Yes, and the reason it's not fired is that it is solid, and there's a good chance that it will explode when it is fired, and so it's in limbo.

JS: [I point to another wing chair.] The pink one is hollow?

LW: No, it's thinner.

HC: It's thinner, and fortunately, it came through the firing okay. But on this one, you can see this hairline crack here. When this is fired higher, that crack will widen, because as the piece shrinks, the two sides here will move away from each other. That will have to be filled with some kind of plaster or clay or epoxy. I see that's going to happen in the bigger chairs, and I don't want to invest a lot of time in doing a figure for those chairs until I can deal with the probability of them going screwy.

JS: Can you fire one chair and see what happens?

HC: That's what I intend to do.

JS: What holds the figure to the chair?

HC: A dowel will be driven the full length of his body and fixed in the couch, or a dowel will protrude from the couch, I haven't decided which. The couch will be glued into the carpet, which is drilled. Those holes go through the clay into the wood.

JS: How do you give the carpet its texture?

HC: You roll out the clay on cloth, on canvas, and then you come back with leather-stamping tools and you do the pattern. But there may be a thousand different stamping actions to get that.

JS: There's a real textile sense to the carpet, and it's not just a plain carpet, it's a thick, deep carpet. Are all of them different?

HC: Most of them are different still. I'm contemplating having decals made, and this is a money versus art argument. I spoke to a licensing agent the other day, and he was trying to explore with me ways of making my work in Taiwan for a mass market. And he's looking and admiring the carpet, and saying, "Oh, that's so great, that would make such a great decal!" In other words, the way he would make the piece, he would have that photographed somehow, and made into a multi-colored decal, and put it on a flat piece of clay, without any handwork, without any depth, only the illusion of depth.

JS: Like Formica.

HC: Exactly. Wood-toned Formica. And I was amazed. It was kind of like I was outside my own body. This was an after-death experience or something. I said, "Gee, Henry, there's not a bead of sweat, there's not a catch in the throat. You've heard that without cringing, without protest."

JS: Now what—

HC: That's maturity!

JS: You think it was maturity and not compromise?

HC: You talk to a young ceramist who's hot, and she's got more orders than she could possibly fill, and you say, you know, you could cast this and hire a helper, and they'll help you unburden yourself from this, and you'll still make the kind of money you deserve to make, as a designer, not as a common laborer. And she would say, "Oh, but all my little fellers have names, and I have to make them by hand." Two years from now, I'll meet her on the way to the bank with an armed guard, and she'll explain to me how she discovered the wonders of casting. It's a matter of gradually losing your virginity, and this is the only way that can be done in stages. With a new idea, you regain your virginity. It doesn't have to be all or nothing.

JS: When I, as an eighty-five-year-old collector, want to buy one of these, I'm going to buy one of these. I'm not going to buy one of the ones that are made like Formica. Isn't there another way?

HC: Aren't Hummels being bought now at prime prices? People are discovering prewar Japan ware. Stuff that was churned out massively before World War II. Look at the pressed glass, the cranberry glass or the blue glass or the milk glass that was given away at movie houses, and now for the price of a plate you could buy eight sets forty years ago. But what the hell, I'm not concerned with posterity. Is anybody putting their money away in the bank against the day when Henry Cavanagh is on the street starving and they're going to give him a $5 bill? So why should I invest my time in an unknown posterity?

JS: Say they license this, then what are you going to do?

HC: I can continue doing it, or I can sit eating lobster tails in Bimini for the rest of my life. That depends on the money.

LW: He can do art pieces. If he sold a couple of his designs, then eventually those pieces would bring him a steady enough income so maybe he wouldn't have to compromise his own work, and maybe he'd have the confidence to ask for the price he deserves for those one-of-a-kind pieces. He wouldn't have to sell himself short.

JS: Why can't you ask for what they deserve?

HC: My bills come in monthly, and my checks have to come in apace. That doesn't happen even now, when I'm underselling. If I had to wait months at a time for a piece to sell, after a while, despair sets in, and I think that affects your work much more adversely than any form of prostitution or cheapening your work does. Galleries conspire wittingly and unwittingly in this. Why go on? There's a great danger in somebody taking another job as a soda jerk.

JS: Do you think that woman would have bought this if it had been $600?

HC: The next thought in my head was, I could have had a higher price on that. I could have come down to $400 ultimately, and she would have thought, wow, he's a great guy, and she'll come to me again. But in the excitement of the moment, I was happy to get what I got. I was just barely paid. I wasn't as well-paid as I would have been if I'd sold $400 worth of butter dishes, that's seven butter dishes.

JS: Which is about twenty-five hours of work.

HC: It doesn't compare, and there's no point in trying to explain it to people because you just make them feel bad and you confuse them. Rembrandt had a factory, Tintoretto had a factory. All these guys took as many commissions as they could possibly scrounge up, against the day when there wouldn't be any. And then, you paint the hat, I'll paint the eyes, you do the clouds, I'll do the shoes. They were working with eight paintings at a time, and people knew that. Four hundred years ago, they were buying the signature. Out of every ten pieces of art that are bought, maybe four people are interested in the content of the work, and all the rest are interested in the signature. You could make something so rare that nobody's interested in it.

LW: I think that in some cases, his hippos are priced so low that people assume they're mass-produced or something, that nobody in his right mind would sell such a piece for that price. A lot of people do not trust their judgement in buying art or craft.

JS: [After a pause] Laura, how do you make your pieces?

LW: This teapot is hand built. [She points to a teapot that is decorated in relief with the figures of small animals. The main feature of the decoration is a bas relief "den" with small faces peeping out of it.] I roll out a slab of clay with a slab roller, then I form the bottom half of the pot around a cylinder.

JS: Is it any particular cylinder?

LW: A Quaker Oats box is what I use. The dome part, I have a plaster form that I made that I press a circle of clay onto. While that top part is setting up, becoming stiff enough, I decorate this bottom portion [with whimsical animal figures] . . .

JS: By application or incision?

LW: These are all applied pieces. I roll out a coil and press it on and smooth it out, and then this texture is [made with] lace, crocheted lace.

I have a bag of stuff I get at yard sales, and [by pressing it into the clay I get] the texture on that hill there. This [texture is made with a] leather stamp, on this other hill. The stains just seep right into every little line, and that gives it a lot of richness and depth. And all these little [animal figures] I shape with my fingers. I'm very dependent on certain tools. I think we all are. Certain tools become useful for making the holes in the ears and cutting away. This arm is an added piece, but I might take a tool to redefine it, because when you press it on, it gets obliterated. These are all done by hand.

JS: This is a little den and this is the outside, the sky . . .

© Jonathan Postma

HC: Laura mentions using a mold, though, and I think it's useful to know that Laura's training is in ceramics and her teachers were very traditional, Japanese-inspired ceramists, and I had no background in ceramics at all. When I came to ceramics through Laura, I didn't have a prejudice against using certain techniques, like casting or decals or slip molding. Laura was aware of those techniques, but I think the teaching emphasis . . .

LW: One teacher used molds almost exclusively, but he assembled parts together. It was not like he had a finished piece from the mold. I had certain biases against molds. I thought of hobby shops. I used to like making the forms by hand. I liked working with the clay. Well, after you've done maybe a hundred of something, there's no fun in it anymore, and the fun is decorating it. I had to find a way to make those tools work for me, and so far, [using some molds] seems to be a good solution.

JS: So, you mold it around the tin, or whatever it is, and then you apply the bottom?

LW: Yeah, the bottom is a circle of clay that I press up over the edge, and the lid is a separate little form. And then this is a strip that I add on.

JS: Is each of these one of a kind?

LW: Sometimes, if I had a lot of these to do, if a lot of shops ordered this size of teapot with bears on it, I might do one and then the next one I might sort of copy, making a few changes, just to get more mileage out of each idea. They're going to different places, and they're going to be painted differently, too.

JS: How much would you sell one of these for?

LW: This sells for $200 and this for $250. That's retail.

JS: And so you're aiming for collectors, too.

LW: Yeah.

JS: Are the mugs cast, too?

LW: I used to do all these by hand, in a similar way to the teapot, but now I'm slipcasting the cup itself, and in this case, the hills are a part of the mold. And then I come back and by hand I model all these add-ons, and press them on. I have to add a little bit more fresh texture, because the texture didn't come out sharply in the mold. I find this slipcasting is really saving me time and boredom, because I really just get to the heart of it now, which is decorating and painting it. Painting is my favorite part. Like Henry said, years ago I would not have considered this, but it also didn't occur to me to cast a form and then add by hand. I always saw it as a total thing. This way I can still have the clarity and the slight differences in the handwork.

JS: If a manufacturer came and bought all your designs, what would you do?

LW: I'm kind of sitting on the fence right now about that. I would like to sell something to an agent to have some kind of royalties coming in on a regular basis. I'm not sure at this point, if I had all the time in the world, without a care about money, I'm not sure what I would do. I would probably drop all of this for a while and just experiment in a different vein in ceramics and see what comes out. I don't feel that I've had that luxury, I haven't felt that in a long time. I've been much more immersed in production-type items, even though they are individual pieces, they're on repeated forms. I really haven't done what I would call show pieces in a long time. Just this February, I got a private commission to do dinnerware for the first time, and that was very exciting for me. It was a huge project—it was a surprise for this guy's wife, for his anniversary. I did sketches, which he approved, and I gave him a general price range, which he approved, and I practically killed myself trying to get it done on time, but they were thrilled with it, and that was very rewarding. Also, it was a real challenge, and it really set me going in a direction that I always kind of wanted to go but didn't know what way to approach it, and I didn't feel I could justify the time.

HC: See, the money was there. In a sense, they paid the tuition for her to learn how to do a dinner set, which is something she should have always been doing. A lot of times, you may be inspired to do something but much of our work is on speculation, and if you've got a hot item, or crashing deadlines, you have to deal with that first, and real play, which is creativity, has to come second.

LW: I took some of these to the fair. I got orders.

HC: Well, the rabbits have always been more popular. To put them in a context where they can be used and seen and admired, it was a great combination. It's one of those things that seems so obvious after you've done it, but she's only been working for ten or twelve years, and hit, hit, hit, but never hitting that. And you never know where an idea is going to come from.

JS: Are these dinnerware pieces cast?

HC: They'll be cast now.

LW: These are press molded. I started with a slab and I pressed them in. I did have a lot of loss. I had to do certainly two for every one that I sent. Most of these plates I had to fire at least twice in a high-firing, because they warped, or they had a tiny glaze flaw that would be very obvious on a big surface like this. I was going nuts. I knew I was going to have problems with the big flat pieces that I hadn't done before, and I just didn't know for a while whether I was really going to come up with the goods.

JS: What were you like when you were doing all this?

LW: I was obsessed with getting the thing done. Was I impossible to live with?

HC: You're never impossible to live with.

LW: I was impossible for myself. I was so anxious, I couldn't sleep at night.

HC: The hard part was the deadline, because she had to manufacture an object that had never been made before, and without knowing what the technological problems would be.

LW: I knew there were going to be some.

JS: How many place settings were there?

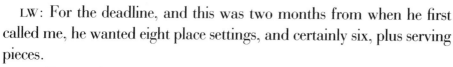

LW: For the deadline, and this was two months from when he first called me, he wanted eight place settings, and certainly six, plus serving pieces.

HC: But on the other hand, the existence of the deadline had its uses, because you might have, if you were doing this as a pure research project—

LW: I could have dragged it out to a year.

HC: You could have dragged it out to a year or you could have abandoned it. You wind up being a total slave to somebody on the other end of a phone line, you've never seen them before. You're doing things for them that you would never do for your family or your friends or yourself. It's the most bizarre way of living!

LW: It is bizarre, and the money, what seemed like an astronomical price originally, seemed like kind of a pittance at the end, because I was working ten or twelve hours a day every day, trying to just refire these things, and you'd have to fire the kiln, which took maybe ten hours to fire and twenty-four to cool.

HC: You know, we used to make our own clay and glazes and all of that, and it was very tedious, and we did it probably because we were poor and we thought we were saving money, but just like the poor have very expensive and bad diets because they buy luncheon meats instead of roast beef, because roast beef is expensive, so they pay $9 a pound for baloney, we were penny wise and pound foolish, in squandering our precious time and talent mixing clay that we could buy. I don't do that anymore but I still have disasters in the kiln. But with Laura's dinnerware, it was something new every time, some quirky thing that you couldn't possibly forecast or take out insurance against. With the figurative work, you're always going to get that, and that's where your cost builds up, because you're on uncharted territory, and you can't schedule that in to some kind of estimated cost. So you go through all that agony, and then you take that work down to a gallery, and you figure your agony is worth $100, and you cross what I call the golden threshold. Miraculously it doubles in value. The gallery is selling it for $200. Two hundred is probably closer to what your agony is worth. It's probably a fair price. It's the wholesale price that's not too fair. But the gallery guy is paying $1,000 a week in rent. When you talk about money and art, that's one of my frustrations. I like doing shows because I think I can sell it at a fair price.

JS: Do you sell it for the retail price at the show?

HC: No. Maybe wholesale plus 20 or 30 percent. A $200 item for $175 or $150, and if they know my work, they figure they're getting a bargain. A lot of artists don't do that, they figure that a show is a opportunity for them to get the retail price that their work has been getting all along.

LW: And the galleries want you to sell at the retail price. You can reach a point where you're doing yourself a disservice. If you're selling wholesale and people know, they might say, well, I can get it from him wholesale, and they'll not go to a gallery, and yet they may not get in touch with you either because they forget about it.

JS: Do you both spend most of your days out here in the studio?

LW: Yeah.

For a moment, in spite of my presence, there is silence, with only the small sounds of paintbrushes on clay. Henry mentions that for this they have been content to live like college students for fifteen years. I look around, and the scene is peaceful. I think what I like is the crowd of tiny figures—Henry's hippos and horses, Laura's rabbits and chipmunks and languid couples—starting down from the racks as if they, too, had plenty of opinions about art and money.

# Graham Blackburn

The chair is the first of what will be twelve. The seat back is tall and narrow. Its central panel, of bright curly maple, is set between two slender stiles of amaranth, a deep purple, very hard wood from Guiana. The headpiece is amaranth, too, inlaid with the merest line of ebony along the top edge. There are no stretchers between the amaranth legs—the chair will depend for sturdiness only upon the strength of its hand-carved mortise and tenon joints. Perhaps because of the high, uncompromising seat back (no loungers at this dining table), the chair has a Gothic air to it. Even so, the lines of construction are clean, exact, perfect-seeming, except to Graham Blackburn, the designer and builder, who looks at it with a critical eye.

Chairs aren't easy to build. Having just built this one, Graham is eloquent on the subject. He says, "The biggest thing about chairs is that despite the fact that we've been the same shape, anatomically, for at least as long as there's been wood-working going on, and so the basic functional shape of the chair doesn't change much, it's really hard to design something small that will be comfortable for us, and also make it structurally strong. The biggest problem with chairs is making them strong enough, and the second biggest problem is that by trying to make them relatively small at the same time, you end up with a design that's got a lot more angles than most other casework. If you look at this chest here, for all its complex-ity, for all the drawers, and all these joints on the side, and all the frame and panel here, all the stuff in the back, everything is square, so you can always measure something from something that already exists. With the chair here, though it looks pretty simple and straightforward, there are a zillion different angles and things. On the back here, there is only one vertical piece. These other pieces slope—this slopes, and then this slopes at a different angle from this, and that is different from the back leg, which flares out. And that's just the back leg. If you look at the rest of the chair, it gets horrendous. The side of the seat is at an angle, and the way this piece joins into the back of the seat is with a mortise and tenon, and those are cut at an angle. Same with the front."

The spare lines of the chair present a further challenge. "It's got to be so exact, or it looks horrible. In older stuff, before they had such exact machinery, they would use a lot of carving and a lot of molding and a lot of panel construction to accommodate wood movement and inac-curacies. But this is total, stripped-down design. If something doesn't fit, you see it immediately. So it's very critical that you can cut that tenon so that it fits right, and then, when you've got this cut out right, you've got to make the hole (the mortise) in there so that it will fit perfectly."

This first chair is actually only the first real chair. Across the room is the mock-up, another chair made from flawed pieces of black walnut as the prototype. After making the prototype, Graham took about a week to make the chair. He says, "That's knowing up front what I was going to build, and having already built that mock-up to get a rough idea of exactly where things were going to go." To finish the eleven chairs still to go, though, he expects to take only three weeks. He says, "Before, it took me all morning to make the pattern, make the shape, to cut it out. Now all I have to do is prepare enough wood all at one go to get all the back legs out of, and then, while the wood is prepared, I can lay that pattern out and mark all twenty-two of them at once." He has a deadline, but even if he didn't, he would produce them that fast, anyway. "What takes the most time is not actually cutting this mortise hole, but marking it, and setting it up in the table, and setting the tool to do it so that it will cut exactly this far in, and exactly this long, and exactly that deep. The actual cutting takes about five seconds."

He used a hand tool, an English mortise chisel, to cut the mortises in the prototype. He places the end of the chisel on the chair leg, and hammers it firmly and quickly with a mallet. He says, "The nature of this chisel is that it has parallel sides and a very thick blade, so it's very strong." The wood comes out in shavings exactly as wide as the chisel. Now, however, since he has so many of them to do, it pays to use a "plunge router"—an electrical machine with a fence to set the spacing. It works rather like a drill. He pushes it down into the wood, pulls it backward, and cuts the slot. He doesn't use the traditional methods out of mere pride, though. He says, "If you're going to do just one, it's just as quick to clamp the wood on the bench and do the old traditional way. If you've got zillions to do, and in each chair there are twelve, it's much quicker to set the machine up, make a special box for the wood to sit in, so it's always in the right position. I only have to make the adjustments once, and then, done."

Graham Blackburn is a tall, bearded man in his mid-forties, almost entirely gray. He speaks with a British accent, somewhat softened by twenty-two years in the United States. His workshop near Woodstock is a large, airy barn, and stands on legendary ground. Just above it, on

© Jonathan Postma

the mountain, was where Bob Dylan used to stay. Legendary or not, the setting is lovely—light, sun-dappled woodland. He likes to work with the two big doors open to the breeze. Being in the workshop doesn't feel entirely like being indoors, and Graham likes it that way. Although he has lived in Woodstock since 1967, he still hasn't adjusted to the winters and is considering a winter move to California, though he would return to Woodstock in the spring.

The walls of the shop are lined with varieties of planes, and he is knowledgeable and eloquent about their origins and uses. He picks up a plane that he found at a yard sale but hasn't had time to clean yet. These early planes, developed in the latter half of the nineteenth century, are made of wood, usually beech, with steel blades. The stock, the wooden body of the plane, is 2 or 3 inches thick, and the blade protrudes through the sole. The stock is intended to wear down—he displays a few that have seen years of use, and their stocks are only about an inch thick—but the blades and other metal parts can easily be reset. Beside the old, apparently unusable plane is another, bright yellow, apparently new, although none of these planes have been manufactured in years. The blade of the first is rusted and dull. The blade of the second is so shiny silver blue that it looks razor sharp. Of course, the second was once in as bad shape as the first. Cleaning up these planes and reseating the hardware is one of Graham's particular pleasures.

Not all of Graham's planes have flat soles, so that in making the chair, and the table (which has rounded ends), he has been able to get the smoothness of planed wood on curved surfaces. These round-soled planes are called compass planes, and a well-equipped cabinetmaker would have an entire selection of them in various curves. He demonstrates, again with the chair. He says, "Probably about the hardest thing about the chair was doing this. And I never did quite find a way of figuring this out. Basically, planing has to be done with the grain. It's like stroking a cat. If you stroke the cat the wrong way, all the fur will bristle up. If you want the wood to be nice and smooth, you plane with the grain. Sometimes, of course, the grain changes direction, so while going in one direction, you're planing with the grain here, at this point, here, you'd be planing against the grain, and risk peeling back the wood. Now that's not too hard a problem if you have really finely tuned cabinetmakers' planes that have tiny, tiny mouths—that's the opening in the sole through which the blade projects. That means it can take a shaving and immediately the shaving is broken by the blade's cap iron, and so it doesn't tear out. You get a smooth cut. If you look at most carpenter's planes, as opposed to cabinetmakers' planes, they've got huge mouths. But even with a cabinetmaker's plane, you should plane with the grain, which can vary on a straight piece of wood. So one of the things that you try to bear in mind when you're making a piece is that you choose the wood so that it will fit the purpose. But when you've got a piece that you need a curve out of anyway, you almost can't avoid the situation that at one point in the curve, you're going to be planing against the grain. The plane to use is a curved plane, but even that needs to be used with the grain. I can plane here, but when I get here, I'd be going against the grain, so I've got to turn around, but in any event, this piece here, above the curve, needs to be straight. But the straight plane won't get into the curve. That was a problem."

What about just using a knife? "A plane is a knife, but it's a knife that's set in a sole that's perfectly flat, and it's the sole that allows the knife to cut perfectly straight. If I were making an old country-style chair, I would use a draw knife. It will cut along nice and straight, but I can also use it to make a curve, and if this weren't such a high-tech piece, I could have used it. In rustic-style furniture, the marks are considered a virtue, but the marks would look out of place on something that relies for its effect on as much smoothness as this."

Although Graham comes from a family of woodworkers—his father was a builder in London—and was trained in school to use and appreciate hand tools, he has only been building furniture as his primary living for about five years. He came to the United States from London to attend Juilliard, and to study music composition. While in New York, he befriended someone who was fond of driving up to Woodstock. He says, "I was living in Greenwich Village, of course, and the place that everybody in Greenwich Village came to in the mid-sixties was Woodstock. That was the only other place in America. What I did while I was going to Juilliard was a lot of music copying and odd bits of waiting tables. At the Figaro Café, where I was a waiter in the Village, there was a guy I became friendly with who had a friend in Woodstock who was going to give him some land. Every Wednesday, Butch would try and come up to Woodstock to meet this guy. They were going to set up some kind of artist's co-op. But since he knew that Wednesday was his day off, Tuesday night, he invariably got very drunk. Wednesday he was in no shape to drive, so for almost the whole summer, every Wednesday I drove him up to Woodstock. At the end of that summer, I remember standing on the village green, and thinking, This is really a neat little town. I could really live here."

He rented a little house for the winter, supported himself by doing carpentry, then lost his apartment in New York. During the spring, he found a piece of land in Woodstock and decided to build a house on it. Though he had never actually built a whole house, he had done enough of the parts, at various times, working in London and elsewhere, that he felt confident about putting together a livable place. "Once you're that familiar with basic wood construction, it isn't that hard. When I got the land and the opportunity to build the house, all it really meant was getting hold of a copy of Architectural Graphic Standards and a couple other books and asking some questions. Read about it at night and do it in the morning. I cut the first tree down on May the first, and on October first, we had to spend our first night there. There was no more money left. I'd borrowed two thousand dollars to do it. That got me the house built, with plastic over the holes where the windows were going to go, and it got a woodstove in there, and a water line, and the septic system, but for the next year or so, it was pretty much pioneer life. Taking water out of the stream and all. I went out and did carpentry that winter, and at the end of every week, if there was five dollars left over from the groceries or whatever, I'd buy a little more wood and put another window frame in or something. Nail by nail."

He also joined a band that was run by "an eccentric philanthropic anarchist," a Bavarian-style brass band specializing in "oompah music," called The Woodchuck Hollow Brass and Woodwind Choir. The founder was Holly Cantine. "He was a wonderful guy," says Graham. "He had no small talk, and he wouldn't look at you when he spoke, so if he had something to say, he'd come up and stand next to you and say it, and then walk away. His main passion was Bavaria, so he wore lederhosen and kept goats, and had this funny old brass band. I joined the band, and it was wonderful to meet all these strange people. The least excuse, we'd be down on the village green, playing for the politicians. Town was so small that a lot of that kind of stuff happened. We weren't getting paid—we almost had to pay them to let us play. But it was a great little social scene."

When Woodstock began to attract musicians as well as artists, Graham began getting work as a musician for local bands, and eventually spent about ten years as a professional musician for rock and roll and blues bands. He played with Maria Muldaur, the Full Tilt Boogie Band, Van Morrison, and other bands. He made some records on his own. After ten years, though, the music business changed and began to pall. In the meantime, Graham had been writing novels and sending them around. Although none of the three sold to a publisher, he became friends with a number of publishers, and one of these, Peter Mayer, then editor-in-chief at Avon books, happened to see the diary Graham had kept of building his Woodstock house. This diary, handwritten and illustrated with line drawings, was eventually published by the Overlook Press, a Woodstock operation, which Mayer's father owned. The resulting book was nicely produced on heavy stock paper.

It sold at a reasonable price, and was, incidentally, profitable. Graham was encouraged by its success to try another, and that one, *The Illustrated Encyclopedia of Woodworking Handtools, Instruments, and Devices*, sold to a publisher just about the same time that Graham's last band was breaking up. In all he has written ten books, nine of them in the same large format, handwritten, with line drawings. Most are about woodworking, but others are about stamp collecting and sailing. By the winter of 1981-1982, he had gotten to the point where he didn't even have to write up a book proposal—he could suggest something he wanted to write about, and sell it for a fair sum. He expected, then, to continue making his living as a writer indefinitely.

The IRS ruling in the fall of 1981 that publishers must pay taxes on their inventory of unsold books changed his plans. Suddenly, three of his books were remaindered, and his advances for new books shrank 90 percent. At the same time, he began noticing changes in the market for fine furniture. "Prices had been creeping up," he says, and had gotten so high that he thought that he could manage to build furniture to his own exacting standards that was better designed and less expensive than the furniture he saw in stores. What had been a hobby and a pleasure became a business. His aim is the high end of the market—people who can afford custom-designed, one-of-a-kind pieces made of exotic woods, people who are as interested in having a "Graham Blackburn" as they are in having something beautiful. The dining table and twelve chairs will go into a New York apartment dining room that is being designed to receive them. The price, as much as a fully equipped conversion van, is breathtaking at first.

But the table took three months to design and build. It is in three pieces, two half circles and a long rectangle. Fully extended, it measures 11 feet long, 4 feet 6 inches wide. The grain of the curly maple inlaid top perfectly matches at the seams between the rectangle and the semicircles. At each corner of each piece is a half leg. When the table is put together, the half legs form perfectly fitted, tapering whole legs. The precision of the fit is emphasized by the ebony inlay in each purple leg. In addition, the table is also designed to function as a smaller round table, 4½ feet in diameter, seating six. The grain of the curly maple matches perfectly at the seam between the two semicircles, as do the half legs, and the six legs of the round table form six neat, aesthetically pleasing slots for six chairs to fit into. A one-of-a-kind piece, with

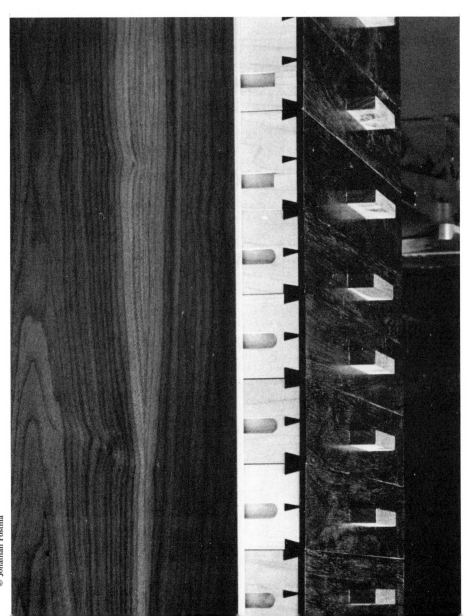

numerous design problems and engineering problems to be successfully worked out, once. The breathtaking price diminishes in grandeur when worked out hour by hour.

In the corner of the workshop stands another piece, a tall, narrow chest about 5½ feet tall and 2 feet wide. It bespeaks, in a less subtle way than the table and chairs, another of the reasons Graham Blackburn spends ten hours a day in his shop. The sides are now of black walnut, the nine drawer fronts of deep, rich, very darkly figured rosewood. When the drawers are opened, the rosewood half of the dovetails contrasts sharply with the shiny smooth maple of the drawer sides. The lower door is a rosewood frame with amaranth panels. Although there is not a scrap of cherry on the piece, it began as a way to use a nice piece of cherry that Graham had been saving in his hoard of wood. A month ago, the black walnut case was suspended between two bright cherry sides. But then he got the urge to use the rosewood, certainly one of the loveliest pieces of wood imaginable, and rare, too. The extremely dark color of the rosewood drawer fronts clashed with the brighter, warmer shade of the cherry, and so the cherry was taken off, and the chest redesigned. He has put hours into the chest, redesigning it, making mistakes, changing his mind, and all in the evenings, after working on the table and chairs.

He says, "It was fun sawing the wood out of the log in there, looking at all the pieces endlessly, so that they all related pattern-wise and color-wise to one another. I'll plane this one more time [the rosewood] and then just wax it. No sandpaper or anything. It's just such wonderful, wonderful wood." He goes to the back of the shop and pulls out pieces of Indian and South American rosewood. They are extremely heavy and dense. Beside them are boards of padauk, cherry, bubinga, pear, all carefully marked. About each variety he has something to say: Bubinga is very hard wood that takes a fabulous polish; pear is beautiful, soft, and mellow, makes very nice, calm pieces; mahogany "works sweetly." "I have all sorts of treasures in here, " he says. "I love the wood. It's hard for me to throw any little pieces away." But he will sell the chest—he has some customers in mind who have already bought a table. It is not owning the wood that interests him, but making something of it.

Or perhaps it is not even that as much as figuring out what can be made. He prides himself on making furniture that is functional. He says, "There is definitely an element of functional craftsmanship that has to be taken into account; otherwise, you're just indulging your aesthetic fancy, if you want to call it that. I look at the shape, the color, and the design. It has to be a pleasant object. Then I'm intrigued by the workmanship—will it do what it's supposed to do as well as look good? And will it do it honestly and well?" Perhaps the rows of antique planes on the wall, in their simple usefulness, represent the ideal as well as the tool. Graham has no children of his own, though he has helped raise two, but he would like to have a school where he would teach hand-woodworking methods to future craftsmen and -women. He waves his hand around the room. "These tools and the methods of using them are so good that I would hate to see them be lost. That's the debt I feel to the older woodworkers; having a school is how I'd like to repay it." He smiles, and I can almost see the students scattered around the shop, bent intently over their work.

# Ward Herrmann

The wood duck on the table looks soft, warm, its feathers rounded and puffed out; the head is cocked; the tail feathers have a stiff delicacy. It is only touch that reveals the hardness of the bird—every feather except the tail feathers is carved from the same block of wood. The care and artfulness of the carving (every barb and shaft of each feather is created with a woodburning tool) have created the optical illusion that a life-size, browny-beige wood duck is floating on the table. The illusion is so convincing that Ward Herrmann, of Delhi, recently won Best in Show at the Mid-Atlantic Waterfowl Festival with the duck, competing against carvers from all over the world. He has been carving decorative decoys and other birds for about four years. He competed as an inter-mediate, but now that he has won, he must compete in the future a professional. In 1985, he won eight ribbons.

Decorative decoy carving is a form of wood sculpture that grew out of the older craft of hunting decoy carving. Ward has done some of that, too. On a low shelf of his workshop, a stylized representation of a harlequin duck rests on a stand. The bright blue harlequin markings are intended to attract other ducks flying overhead, and the keel along the base of the duck is intended to keep the decoy upright. These decoys are simply designed to enable the owner to use them year after year and repaint them as necessary, and to hold down the amount of labor a craftsman must put into them, and therefore the cost, since the hunter must buy as many as two dozen of them. And it is true that ducks flying overhead are not especially discriminating, not, for example, as discriminating as Ward Herrmann, who carves decoys with the same pleasure, and for the same reasons, that he paints wildlife paintings and makes watercolors of songbirds and covered bridges.

The raw material is basswood, or maybe tupelo gum. Both woods are soft and light, because the decorative decoys, though they will never be used for hunting, will be judged in shows for floating characteristics. Once, in the early days, Ward took a bird to a show, and after only a few seconds in the water, it was disqualified. The judge later told him that its floating balance was off by 3 degrees. Some of Ward's decoys are hollow, some are solid. All now float horizontally to the surface of the water, as ducks do. He has carved many breeds of duck—widgeons, canvasbacks, pintails, mallards. The models range around the walls of the shop, birds he has shot and had mounted by taxidermists. The aim, with the decoys, is not self-expression but precision—the kind of exact appreciation of nature that comes from recreating a natural form.

The first step is to make a roughly carved block of wood that resembles the shape of the duck. The head, like the tail feathers, will be made from a separate piece and attached. Even at this first step, Ward is as precise as possible, aware of this details in the duck he intends to make;

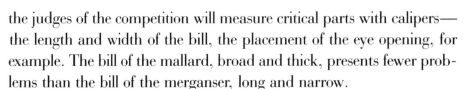

the judges of the competition will measure critical parts with calipers—
the length and width of the bill, the placement of the eye opening, for
example. The bill of the mallard, broad and thick, presents fewer problems than the bill of the merganser, long and narrow.

After cutting out the rough shape, Ward takes the wood to his grinding table where, with a tool that looks as if it belong in a dentist's office,
a foredom, he grinds and sands the contours of the duck's body into the
wood. Although he has drawn a few lines on the wood to indicate where
the wings and the base of the neck will come, he works mostly by eye,
from long experience with birds of all types. Then he does the same
with the head, smoothing in the contours of the eyes, the roundness of
the crown, the arch of the neck, the contours of the bill. Though the
grinder is electric, the work is not quick, and Ward estimates that he
spends some thirty to forty hours shaping slowly with the grinder—
never grinding away too much, always aiming for that soft, living figure. He puts in the eyes, taxidermist's eyes, careful to measure the
eyeholes exactly.

You could say that now the work begins, the work of giving the bird
a realistic surface. Ward glues the head to the body, and then sets about
texturing the whole bird, feather by feather, with a finely pointed electrical woodburning tool. When the bird is painted, it is the tiny grooves
that will create the illusion of real feather texture under the coat of the
paint. The most important thing about drawing the feathers on the
wood is imagining the way water would flow over them, and making
their pattern convincingly hydrodynamic. He works quickly, freehand,
sometimes turning the animal one way or another. The feathers grow
under his hand—tiny ones around the base of the beak and the eyes,
larger about the neck. Along the back, where the large feathers of the
wings lay across one another, the woodburning tool becomes a sort of
carving tool. He works into the wood under the feathers, separating
them from the rest of the bird. Then he works on each of these flight
feathers individually, aware that no feather is uniform—all have high

spots and low spots, variations in texture and shape. It is the realistic variations that create the ideal duck.

Ward also carves a lot of feather pins ("bread and butter," he calls them), and so he is adept at creating that particular illusion, the illusion that something hard, wood, is something soft, a feather. It is the feathers along the backs of his ducks that demand to be touched, just to check. They seem as delicate and slender as the real thing, overlapping and crossing one another as if carved individually, but nonetheless carved as a single piece.

Of course, the painting is as painstaking as the burning in of the feathers. Ward uses acrylic paints and mixes his own colors to match the colors of his models. He uses a variety of fine-tipped sable brushes, and paints each feather on, a barb at a time. The burned-in lines serve as a guide for the brush. Ducks are, in fact, very colorful animals. Even a female mallard exhibits numerous variations of shade between brown and beige, and these variations must be carefully rendered. He begins with the head, painting on the lighter base colors, then gradating washes of darker colors, once again doing the work freehand, only occasionally pausing to glance at the model. He is an experienced painter, so the work goes rather quickly. He has set himself the task of painting two birds for a single customer in the space of about two weeks. He works a ten-hour day in his shop. Last year, he had commissions for nineteen carved birds and ten paintings, and this year he looks forward to contracting for about the same amount of work. He is independent enough to take on only projects he wants to do, and well-known enough among hunters and collectors that he is never without work.

Life-size decoys aren't the only birds Ward carves. He does songbirds, owls, geese, and turkeys, although these aren't life-size. What he likes to do with turkeys, a game bird plentiful in Catskill forests, is construct tableaus to scale. One of his first is displayed in his studio— two turkeys, their wattles bright red, their feathers dark and iridescent,

are walking in the autumn beside a shallow trickle that runs along the forest floor. Miniature red and yellow maple and beech leaves lie in the stream bed and are strewn about in the mud. Protruding cedar roots separate the two turkeys. Every element of the scene is artificial. The leaves are made of paper with the veins burned into them. The stream is a clear epoxy resin. The bodies and heads of the turkeys are wood, their legs wire, solder, and epoxy. It took Ward 39½ hours to make each pair of legs. It took him 500 hours to complete the entire sculpture.

Into each of these pieces goes a certain amount of what might be called engineering. Ward intends, soon, to begin a sculpture that a customer has commissioned, of a pintail drake in flight, wings spread, feet extended for landing. Some cattails will be a part of the scene, and one of the cattails will be painted steel, a base for mounting the flying pintail by its wing. The stresses on the piece will be large ones: The wingspread of the bird will be about 39 inches. A trained engineer and tool designer as well as artist, Ward looks forward to these sorts of challenges.

Ward has been painting almost his whole life. His first commission, for a series of songbirds, came to him when he was thirteen. How did he familiarize himself with the anatomy and coloring of the birds? He gives a rare wry chuckle. "Well," he says, "There's only one way, and that's have a bird in your hand." He has been painting continuously since then, not only, not even especially, wildlife. He has done domestic animals, hunting dogs, portraits, murals. One of his murals is a picture of a navy ship task force in battle formation. Another is of James Bay, with ducks and geese migrating and coming in. Another is in Palo Duro State Park, in Texas. He has done landscape and still life, in oil, acrylic, watercolor (his favorite medium and, according to him, the most diffi-cult, since the painter can't correct mistakes), pastel, and pencil. He has also mastered quite a few other disciplines—he put himself through college at Buffalo State Teachers' College (now SUNY Buffalo) by designing tools for Curtis Wright, a local firm, in the evenings, and then worked in the navy during World War II as a machinery designer. He has designed jewelry for Gump's, taught costume design, package design, stage design. After the war, he set out to learn every craft and then to teach them all, and he spent most of his working life teaching, then directing the department of Art and Design at the State University of New York at Delhi.

Some years ago, he also turned to filmmaking. He and two friends decided to make films of light tackle fly-fishing in remote parts of the world. He says, "We'd pick out a spot on the map where a river came out of a lake, in Northern Quebec or Northwest Territories. Some places, they had to fly gas in and cache it in order for us to get into where we wanted to go." It was exciting, but Ward says, "The movie industry is just like the diamond industry, it's controlled by a very few people, and when you go to sell, you've got to take what they offer you, or else you won't sell. We put too much time into it for the amount of money we were getting out of it." Ward got out of the business, but many of the paintings hanging on the walls are of these wild, barren places.

Another project that has been an act of love is the book Ward wrote, illustrated, designed, and published in 1974, entitled *Spans of Time; Covered Bridges of Delaware County, N.Y.* It is a large-format (12 × 17½) history of the early days of Delaware County, which uses the fifty-seven covered bridges that Ward discovered had once spanned the county's streams as a focus for other, more widely ranging reminiscences of county life, notable characters, and traditional methods of building and going about daily tasks. Each of the fifty-seven bridges is the subject of a drawing or a painting. Ward did the research and managed to uncover a great deal of descriptive material about the bridges—drawings or, often, photographs taken just before the bridges fell down or were taken down to make way for steel or concrete bridges. There is a drawing on nearly every page, not only of bridges, but of old buildings (the old stone schoolhouse at Dunraven Station, the creamery near Austin's bridge, Arkville), old forms of transportation (two oxen yoked to a wagon, a steam locomotive, a raft-type ferry), old machinery (a butterchurn powered by a treadmill, iron knuckles from Anti-rent War days, found south of Andes, a cradle scythe), old scenes (a man with a dancing bear, a man driving turkeys to market, a panorama of Delhi, nestled in the hills). The text is folk history—tales of old-timers and old ways lost to more formal histories. The project took Ward four and a half years of intense work. It was printed by the Intelligencer Press, in Pennsylvania, the press Ward considered to be the best in the country, and it has won a number of awards. Of the 3,500 copies printed, only 780 still remain. After the first printing, Ward destroyed the plates, although there are prints of some of the paintings in the book that Ward had reproduced separately and laminated as placemats. He has not been persuaded to follow the book with another, but he is glad he did it and proud of the result.

He says, "What got me to do the book to start with was that they built these two reservoirs, and that eliminated a lot of the bridges and also eliminated a lot of the people along the rivers whose great-grandfathers settled this countryside, made the farms, and cleared them off. They were pushed out, and no one was making any attempt to record any of this. At every town along the rivers was a covered bridge, or sometimes more than one. The Covered Bridge Society of New York State was only aware of twenty-nine of them. They had photographs of twenty-eight of them. I found fifty-seven sites and photographs of forty-six of them. I would take photographs that people had of people, and incorporate them into the photographs of the bridge, so all the people in the pictures were real people around here." It is a fascinating book, locally famous in the Catskills for its beauty and its wealth of information.

A passion closely connected to his passion for making paintings and sculptures is his love of the outdoors. He has hunted enthusiastically since boyhood, mainly with bow and arrow, though now, more and more, with a camera. Of turkey hunting, his favorite, Ward says, "They're pretty sharp. They have tremendous eyesight. They're much harder to kill than a white-tailed deer." Ward killed his first deer and his first turkey in the same year, 1939. Good sportsmanship in turkey hunting is part of the hunting laws, but not all the hunters abide by those. The trick is to lure the turkeys out of the trees, where they roost at night—it is illegal to kill them before dawn, or while they are roosting. The hunter installs himself a fair distance from the turkeys, and then calls them, either by voice or with a mechanical turkey call. The call can sound like a hen turkey crying out, or a whole flock of turkeys commenting upon something. The hunter sits very still, and when the turkeys get within range, the hunter has a shot. Now Ward mostly likes to call the game in order to photograph it, but he will still shoot a large bird if he needs the meat. He likes the meat. "They're delicious. They make a tame turkey taste like nothing. You can take a wild bird—you'd have to cook it slow, four or five hours, but when you get through, it's delicious. Good smoked, too." He also takes younger hunters out, in which case he takes a gun rather than a bow, so that there will be no risk of wounding the game and being unable to kill it. He deplores the way ignorant or unskilled hunters shoot at the turkeys roosting in the trees. "I can owl hoot in the morning [he demonstrates], and the bird will gobble back at me in the spring from the roost in the tree, when it's still dusky—semidarkness. I'll walk in and get fairly close to that bird and then I'll call again, and then I'll get about 150 yards away, and wait for it to get light. Then I'll make a fly-down call, and I'll call those birds down and over to me. These fellows, they'll walk right in and over to the roost. They can see them silhouetted against the sky—they don't care whether it's a hen or a gobbler. They shoot them, and they've gotten a turkey. Big deal. Some sportsmanship."

The entire hunting culture of the Catskills has changed with the influx of absentee landowners and absentee hunters. Absentee land-owners are more likely, whether they hunt or not, to post their land against trespassing. Some absentee hunters are likely to trespass and do damage. The old custom, which Ward still abides by, of asking permission of the landowner, and then thanking the landowner by bringing him a bird or some other present, is less prevalent, and less possible, since many of the landowners are elsewhere. According to the Catskill Mountain News, some 55 to 60 percent of the land in Delaware County is owned by people who live outside the county, up from almost none a generation ago. One thing Ward likes to do as a return is prune and trim wild apple trees, so that they begin to produce again. Hunters from elsewhere are more likely to view the land as some sort of public domain, available for whatever they want to do with it. Ward tells of an incident he read about in the Binghamton newspaper—a fisherman got permission from a farmer to fish on his land. The next weekend, he returned, without permission, with three carloads of his friends. When the farmer found them fishing and picnicking, he expressed anger and asked the intruders to leave, and he also noted the fisherman's license plate number. The next weekend, he gathered together some firewood, a picnic basket, and his family, went to Binghamton and had a picnic on the fisherman's front lawn, barbecue and all. When the homeowner came storming out, the farmer said, "Well, you did this down on our place, why can't we do it on your place?"

He goes on, "You see a lot of examples of poor sportsmanship. A lot of the city hunters, if they don't get a shot, they'll take a shot at anything else, a red squirrel or a bird, anything. They have no concern about what's behind it, where the bullet's going to go. It's hard to believe. This year, eight times, when I was calling in wild turkeys, I had men try to move in between me and the bird and get a shot at the bird. They just scared them away." He isn't sanguine. "With the overuse of land, it's going to come to the situation they have in Europe—unless you own a big area or belong to a club, the only place you'll be able to hunt is on state land." The population of the game has changed, too. "It used to be," says Ward, "that if you went out just before opening day, in the evening, you could see from twenty to forty deer in a meadow. Now you're lucky to see two."

Ward gets invited to hunt all over the country by admiring hunters who appreciate his work, and he has done some hunting in other parts of this country and Canada, but now he prefers to stay in the Catskills where, he says, the altitude is healthy and the air is clean. Clean air gets increasingly important. Perhaps as a result of years of inhaling paint fumes and other fumes, he has a chronic respiratory ailment, and it looked, for a while, as though he was going to have to give up carving, a fume-filled, dusty business. His response was to remodel his shop rather along the lines of a nuclear fuel lab: Every operation has its own table, and each table is encased in clear plastic. Ward sits down and puts his hands through the holes and does his work. Suction fans inside the table draw away the sawdust immediately. Another larger fan can clear the air of the whole shop in one minute. He says, "Still can't eliminate the dust a hundred percent, but you can do the best you can."

The Catskills have always attracted painters and hunters. Before the Revolutionary War, and before Thomas Cole and John James Audubon, painters and printmakers tried to capture the compelling beauty of the region's mountains and valleys and waterfalls and cloudscapes. As much as any of these, at the latter end of this long tradition, Ward Herrmann makes his record of the Catskill Mountains in our day. Feather by feather, duck by duck, brushstroke by brushstroke, he creates a whole landscape of birds and animals and plants and citizens; he simultaneously memorializes a culture that he fears is being lost and helps it to survive. Through his work the quality of diversity that is so marked about life in the Catskills—diversity of plant and animal life, diversity of landscape, diversity and changeability of the weather, of the seasons, of the human population and its endeavors—is expressed in detailed and specific birds and bridges and human faces. It is a record that all who love the Catskills, who wish, with flytier John Hoeko, to be "cemented to this planet," must be grateful for.

# The Quilters

I am sitting with five other women in a large room, white with the brilliant sunshine that pours in. Thick oak beams crisscross above our heads, and the tall windows give us a view of dark green mountains in every direction. Sometimes we look up and out, but mostly we pay attention to our stitches. Under our twelve hands is a patchwork quilt, a giant Around the World, with a flying geese border. The quilting pattern is a simple one—parallel lines of stitching, about 1½ inches apart. The fabric is too dark to mark, so we lay masking tape against already stitched lines, and then stitch beside it. The quilting is in white thread, so that when we turn over the quilt and look at the back, the quilting itself forms an austere, pleasing, abstract pattern on white against blue.

We are talking about gallstones. One of the quilters is absent—she has taken her husband, who was suffering from intense pain, to the local hospital, and no one knows yet what has happened or how he has been diagnosed. Majority opinion around the table is gallstones—that's the kind of pain it was, others have been known to have it. After gallstones, the talk turns to cataracts. One of the quilters will be going into the hospital soon to have a cataract removed, and she is frightened. Although she has only alluded to her fear once, we all know that it is deep and constant. The hospital is in Kingston, forty miles away. Anything could happen there. She will be far away from home.

Someone says, "Have you ever seen one?"

"What?"

"A cataract. I saw some once, in a jar. They're hard and milky, like little buttons."

We take this in. Always we keep stitching. Quilting stitch is a basic basting stitch, as small as possible. The thread is thick and covered with wax to make it stiff. Purists quilt only in white. The needles are called *betweens*. They are short, sharp, and easy to manipulate around a curve. The goal of technique is both speed and fine stitches. Quilts, after all, are practical items, for throwing over beds and keeping warm under. One stitch at a time isn't enough. Two is okay, three is good, and four is a little ostentatious. Inch by inch, we make our way along the lines that have been marked on the quilt. The talk is still of diseases. Hypothyroidism, this time. One of the symptoms is fear. The patient in question, the daughter of one of the women, is always afraid. But she is on medication. She will recover. The trick is not to avoid all these diseases—they can't be avoided. That is the understanding around the table. The trick is to recover.

I cut another thread, put the end through the eye of the needle, tie a single knot in it. The way to hide the knot is to pull the thread through the fabric, then scratch the fabric lightly with a fingernail, aligning the weaving again. After that, I pull gently on the end close to the knot, until the knot is just under the fabric. Then I snip off the end about a half an inch from the knot, and pull the knot, with the needle, the other way. The knot is now nestled between the three layers of top, batting, and backing that form the quilt. When I finish stitching with this thread, all I do is turn and go backward, covering as exactly as I can three of the stitches I have already taken. Then I draw the thread through the fabric at an angle, pull it so that it puckers the fabric slightly, cut close to the puckered fabric. When I smooth it out with my fingertips, the thread end disappears.

Sometimes, because the son of one of the women is a highway patrolman, we talk about accidents out on Route 28. Route 28 runs from Kingston to Margaretville, where it turns sharply toward New Kingston, and then on to Oneonta and points northward. It is two lanes, and curves between the mountains. An interesting collection of eateries lines it, especially around Shandaken. The drive from the Kingston-Rhinecliff bridge west is always lovely, even in the rain, when gray scarves of clouds float just above the dark black-green of the wet, forested hillsides. But it is smooth and dangerous, easy to speed on, with repeated sudden turn-offs and hidden driveways. The accidents are sometimes spectacular—a car ripped in half, people staggering around on the road, an explosion of dust hanging in the air.

But the theme of our quilting meetings isn't always stitches and death. Not too long ago, one of the members made a big sale to the Museum of Modern Art. She had a hundred thousand movie stills from the thirties and forties, all neatly catalogued and stored in her garage in Halcott Center. When a number of the studios got rid of their collection of old stills in the early fifties (God knows why they *gave* them away) Lilo got them—big satin-covered albums of Clark Gable and Vivien Leigh. Now she has made a deal with the Modern. The sum is undisclosed, even around the quilting frame, but it is enough that she can invite all of us out to brunch at one of the local tablecloth restaurants. Her dog barks. He is tied outside the back door. Soon we will break for lunch. Everybody brings her own, and someone brings the dessert.

This week, Eleanor, who has lived in the Catskills since she was born, brings the last of her iceberg lettuce. You can eat it without dressing, it is so crisp and flavorful. Eleanor and I talk about how the Catskills are good for growing lettuce and spinach, but some years the tomatoes never ripen.

When I sit with the quilters, I always ask where they live. "Dry Brook Road," "Little Redkill Road," "Pine Hill," "back near Mill-brook." They are dispersed over the landscape, dispersed over the political spectrum, the ethnic spectrum, the age spectrum. They disagree from time to time about the aesthetic pleasures of this or that quilt, or whether the border of a quilt should be quilted with, say, discreet groups of overlapping hearts or a continuous line of them. What they all share is the urge to make things. When they are not at the quilting group, they are home knitting sweaters or tailoring clothing or working up stuffed Christmas ornaments for crafts fairs. Or writing books. I am happy when I am with them, and it seems to me that they are happy, that perhaps the mere action of pulling stitches through fabric is a soothing one, that the way the colorful quilt under our hands contrasts with the white walls of the room we are sitting in enters and pleases each of us.

Yes, I fall prey to the image, the traditional American image of women at a quilting bee, homemade art, homemade bed covering, homemade pleasure. And to the other traditional American image— anyone can come, anyone can stitch. Some of us have accents, some of us don't, some of us were born 5 miles down the road, some of us were born abroad, some of us were born on the other coast. Some of us live in Fleischmanns, where on Saturday it is common to see the Hasidim strolling, deliberate, up and down Main Street. Some of us live in Mar-garetville, a mere 6 miles from Fleischmanns, where it is already up-state New York, and people are blonder and speak with a flatter accent, where hunting is a commoner pastime than strolling.

A few years ago, Nancy Smith, who is the president of this group, and who was born and raised in Pine Hill, where she still lives, started The Catskill Mountain Quilters' Hall of Fame. It now numbers about twenty members, of various ages, but she started it to recognize the lifework of Catskill women who were making beautiful quilts, and had been for sixty or seventy years. Quilting is as traditional in the Catskills as it is in the Southern Appalachians, so traditional that Catskill quilters are a little suspicious of southern techniques and craftsmanship—when I mentioned, last summer, that I was going to North Carolina and would be looking out for quilts, there was a lot of head shaking at the table. Big, uneven stitches was what I would find there. I felt a little defensive when I got back and reported that I had seen many beautiful quilts. "Mmm" was the only comment anyone made. Perhaps I hadn't looked closely enough was what went unsaid.

Nancy asks me if I have finished the two quilt squares I agreed to make for the pastel quilt the group is making to sell. I haven't, actually, though I am making good progress on the trumpet vine square I've copied from Ruby McKim's book, *101 Quilt Patterns*. Until last night, I was making great progress, but last night, just before I was about to sew together the last seam, I measured the square and discovered that it was nearly 18 inches across rather than 16½. And then, an hour and a half later, after I had ripped a number of seams and sewn them back together, cutting a few pieces down to reduce the size of the square, I discovered that I had cut one of the pieces exactly ¼ inch too much, along the seam line rather than along the cutting line. I could even remember doing it, cosying the crotch of the scissors right up to the wrong line and not thinking twice before making the cut. I was singing along with the radio. Since the piece was already sewn on five sides (it was an octagonal piece) to other pieces, that was five seams that had to come out and go back in again. What I did was stop singing along with the radio and pause to count the number of pieces in the trumpet vine square. There were seventy-two. After that I went to bed.

"It's all in the cutting," says Elsa, who is sitting across the Around the World quilt from me. "Piecing is all in the cutting. And you can't cut one layer at a time, either. You have to have good sharp scissors and cut at least four layers at a time. One layer doesn't have enough body." It's true. I was just a shade careless about the exact size of the seam allowances, and my generosity in cutting them too large added up, over seventy-two pieces, to a square that was 1½ inches too large.

"Pressing, too," says Arlene. "You have to press every seam as soon as you sew it or you won't sew the next ones right."

Privately, I console myself that my talent is in design. But their talents are in design, too, as the annual quilt show that is to begin next week will attest. One top, made by Eleanor, is cream with pink and blue calico oak leaves appliquéd in ranks—as simple as possible, but striking and unusual. Another, a finished quilt designed and executed by Lilo, takes its inspiration from a piece of velvet from the thirties— the colors are shades of gold and rust, and they radiate in widening spokes from off-center yellow suns. These many sunsets seem to overlap one another, creating a wild, urban, sophisticated pattern. Four quilts done by Nina, who is eighty-nine and no longer comes to meetings but still quilts at home, are each more brilliant than the last. My favorite is a pattern of brilliant green leaves and vines appliquéd with equally brilliant purple grapes on a pure white background. Another is neither pieced nor appliquéd, but all cross-stitched, in delicate pastels, as different in effect from the grapes as possible. There will be 50 to 60 quilts in the show, mostly made by these women (with a few from their personal collections). The display piece of the show will be the Jazz Quilt, black on white, a big grand piano in the middle and various other instruments about the edge, designed by Nancy and made by the others, to be raffled off at a jazz festival in the fall. It is stylish and stark, about as American, and as far from early American, as a quilt could get.

We all are faithful to the Monday quilters' meeting. The only excuses anybody really makes have to do with babysitting (lack of) or illness (presence of). In the winter, Elsa had her hip joints replaced, and Evadine is not the only member to experience cataract surgery. I know why we come, why quilting, although repetitive and time-consuming, generate not despair, like other repetitive and time-consuming tasks such as riveting bolts in an auto factory, but peace. That is, I don't know it with my head, but I know it with my hands. Two or three hours move with calm and deliberate speed, measured out in a row of hearts stitched, or the parts of an appliquéd square outlined. Unlike the rest of life, these hours seem to pass neither with a feverish, exhilarated quickness nor with tedious lag. Adrenaline does not pump. The conversation falls silent from time to time, gives way to the small, comforting sound of thread being drawn through fabric. In the silence, there is no pressure for the conversation to begin again. This is not a dinner party. The only necessary communal activity is stitching, and so there is as much time to ponder one's own thoughts as there is to communicate them. Those thoughts, even if they are painful, seem to adopt the quiet order of the stitching—they seem to move forward, not to be locked in neurotic circles, and they seem to approach insight, rather than to rush headlong toward revelation.

I love quilting and hand sewing. Part of the reason my trumpet vine square is taking so long is that it is all hand-stitched rather than machine-stitched. These days, even the purest of the pure piece on the machine, but I don't, because the sewing machine drives me crazy. I can't think of a time when I have tried machine sewing that I haven't fallen into a reverie about old injuries and slights done to me by the most distant and innocent of acquaintances. It is like a trance—the whir of the machine, the catalogue of unrevenged wrongs. After a couple of hours, when I make my first real mistake, for example discovering that I have cut two left sleeves, my first response is to leap from my chair, ready and eager to shed blood. Hand-sewing has the opposite effect. I think of nothing at all in a systematic way. I just stick the needle in, push it with the thimble, and admire what I've done. I sing along with the radio, I press the seams. Nearly every craftsperson I spoke to has the exact same feeling. Some say they are "high," some say they just feel good, or are happy. For all, if my experience serves me, the work is a kind of physically paced meditation not much different from purely spiritual meditation. That is why, perhaps, when I discovered the mistakes I had made in my square, I was neither frustrated nor disappointed, only aroused, as if from sleep. Frustration might have been the next step, but one thing I noticed about all the craftspeople I spoke to, compared to the people I know who don't regularly make things, was their patience.

It makes humans so happy to have their hands on objects that perhaps there is some chemical in the brain that is generated by ordered movements of the fingers. A cup, a chest, a glass vase, a quilt, all of these ask to be touched, and in the natural course of use are touched repeatedly. In fact, most useful objects are experienced in a variety of ways—a cup of tea is warm in the hands and fragrant as well as, possibly, beautiful or interesting. A finely made table is smooth and cool, of a handsome color, comfortable to sit at, laden with food that smells good and tastes good. Even when the object is being ignored, it is present.

Large crafts fairs such as the American Crafts Council Fair, at West Springfield, Baltimore, and San Francisco, or the Rhinebeck Fair, on the Dutchess County Fairgrounds, are the public's main experience of fine craft. The size and sophistication of these fairs, with craftspersons from all over the nation, and work that would otherwise be found at Tiffany's or Bergdorf's, attests to the strength of the crafts movement in our time. Graham Blackburn, Laura Wilensky, and Henry Cavanagh are typical participants in these fairs, in that they bring a great deal of education and style to their work. Even fairs in more traditional regions, such as the Southern Highlands Handicrafts Guild Fair in Asheville, North Carolina, do not display much folk art. By 1986, fifteen years into the crafts movement, enough artisans have been to art school, and enough have perfected their techniques, so that primitive is nowhere to be found. The crafts fairs are full of beautiful objects and expert craftpersons, who have discovered that the price of expertise is production, and production out in the studio isn't much different from production in any other sort of factory.

Discussion around the quilting frame turns to last week's quilt show down in Kingston, where we went as a group. The subject of the discussion is the second most expensive quilt at the show, a quilt entitled *Unwinding the MBA*. The pattern formed a complicated spiral, beginning in the lower left quadrant with the full right side of a vest, and then whirling outward, using suit jacket sleeves, collars, pockets. The spiral unwound into casual shirt materials and faded blue denim. Great use was made of men's ties, and onto the border were sewn countless black silk suit labels. Its price, $4,500, sparks a long discussion about its value that could be taking place in any academic art appreciation class. All the women agree that they wouldn't have it on the bed. All the women agree that it wasn't beautiful. All the women agree that it was beautifully made—fine stitches, excellent overall workmanship. What they can't agree on was the source of its value. Those who like the quilt find it interesting and value it for that. Those who hate the quilt find it ugly and devalue it for that. Other quilts from the show are mentioned as being more desirable, though less expensive, and it turns out, of course, that each of us was struck by a different pattern. We fall silent, as little able to persuade the other tastes as anyone ever is. We also continue to stitch, snip, make knots, hide knots, and I think that for me, it is the continuity of the work that is the value of quilting, and of craft. Use, after all, uses things up. A fifty-year-old quilt is an old quilt. A fifty-year-old painting is a young painting.

It is no coincidence that we often talk of mortality and disease around the quilting frame. We are not separated from our lives by coming here, and regular gatherings often take on ritual qualities. In addition to that, regular meetings make us friends as well as co-workers. But I feel something else here—I feel that the stitches themselves are a positive assertion against mortality as well as tangible evidence that time is being put to good use. We talk about mortality here because we think about it elsewhere, and because here, together, with our hands on the substance of the world, it is safe enough to talk about it.

Arlene says she has to leave, and Nancy reminds her that her turn for dessert is next week. Evadine always comes with Arlene, and so Arlene says, "Ready, Evadine?" A few moments later, glancing at their going through the window, Elsa says she needs to get to the bank before it closes. She gets up. "Well," says Eleanor, "I guess it is time." The inevitable moment has arrived, and so, before too many have left, we take the framed quilts off the stands and lean them against the wall, where they are huge and bright and arresting. Nancy puts away the thread and the tea bags. Lilo goes out the back door and can be heard ordering her dog to stay down, get down. Nancy pauses to talk to someone, and I go out alone, into the clear Catskill afternoon. Across Route 28, Dry Brook Ridge is nearly blue. Wildflowers bloom in every waste spot—daisies, black-eyed Susans, wild chicory. I have been leaning over all day, and so I lift my shoulders and arch my back. How lucky we are.